FRANCHISE LAW
DECODED

FRANCHISE LAW DECODED

THE ESSENTIAL LEGAL GUIDE FOR FRANCHISE SUCCESS

ATTORNEY HOUSTON BARNES

Drifting Seas
Publishing

Cover design by Kristen Andrews, Creative Director at Hachette Book Group
Cover copyright © 2024 by Houston Barnes

First Printed October 2024

Library of Congress Control Number: 2024920914

ISBN: 9798991641807 (hardcover), 9798991641814 (ebook), 9798991641821 (paperback)

For more information or to arrange for Houston Barnes to appear on a podcast, speak at an event, or participate in other engagements, please contact: houston@houstonbarnes.com.

Printed in the United States of America

FIRST EDITION

———

To the Franchise Family of Professionals working everyday to help people realize their dreams.

———

CONTENTS

RESOURCES

INTRODUCTION

WHY LEGAL KNOWLEDGE MATTERS FOR FRANCHISEES

FRANCHISING is one of the most powerful and proven ways to grow a business. For many aspiring entrepreneurs, buying into an established franchise brand seems like the ideal path to business ownership. After all, you're not starting from scratch—you're investing in a proven system with built-in name recognition, operational support, and established products or services. But as with any major business decision, there's more to the story.

As an attorney who has spent years working in the world of franchising, I can tell you that while the opportunity can be rewarding, but is not free from risk. Franchising is, at its core, a legally bound relationship. The contract that you sign—commonly known as the franchise agreement—will define everything from the royalties you'll pay to the territories you can operate within. Understanding that agreement, as well as the many other legal documents and obligations that come with it, is crucial to your success.

And here's where many would-be franchisees fall short.

Many franchisees sign agreements without fully understanding what they're committing to. Often, they assume that since the franchisor has developed a successful business model, there's no need to dig into the details. But this is where problems can arise. A franchisor's business success does not guarantee that the terms of the agreement are in your favor. In fact, franchise agreements are often structured to protect the franchisor's interests, sometimes at the expense of the franchisee.

This book is designed to level the playing field. Whether you're new to franchising or already own multiple franchise units, understanding the legal framework that governs your business is key to making informed decisions. As a franchise attorney, I've seen countless situations where a lack of legal knowledge has led to avoidable disputes, financial hardship, and sometimes even business failure. My goal is to help you avoid those pitfalls by giving you the tools and knowledge to navigate the legal aspects of franchising with confidence.

In this book, we'll cover everything you need to know about the legal side of franchising—from deciphering the Franchise Disclosure Document (FDD) to negotiating favorable terms in your franchise agreement. We'll dive into operational issues, such as how to handle territory restrictions, royalty fees, and marketing obligations. We'll also explore what happens when things go wrong—whether that's a dispute with your franchisor, a potential termination of your franchise agreement, or planning for an exit from the franchise altogether.

By the end of this book, you'll have a clear understanding of the franchise relationship and the legal obligations that come with it. You'll learn how to spot red flags in franchise agreements, how to avoid common legal mistakes, and how to leverage legal knowledge to protect your investment and maximize your success.

Because the truth is this: franchising is about more than just following a business plan. It's about navigating a legal relationship that will define the way you do business. Understanding that relationship will help you take control of your future as a franchise owner.

Let's get started.

PART I

THE FRANCHISE CONCEPT AND INITIAL STEPS

1

UNDERSTANDING THE FRANCHISE BUSINESS MODEL

The world of franchising offers an exciting opportunity for those seeking to become business owners without starting from scratch. But to fully grasp the potential of franchising, it's essential to understand what it is, how it works, and what makes it different from other business models. While franchising presents unique benefits, it also comes with specific challenges and responsibilities that prospective franchisees must be prepared to navigate. This chapter will break down the franchise business model, explaining its key components, the roles of the franchisor and franchisee, and the pros and cons of this type of business arrangement.

What is a Franchise?

A franchise is a legal and commercial relationship between the owner of a business system (the franchisor) and an individual or entity (the franchisee) who purchases the right to operate a business under the franchisor's brand and according to its operational guidelines. Simply put, franchising is a way for the franchisor to expand its brand and business model while allowing franchisees to run their own businesses under that established brand.

. . .

THE FRANCHISE MODEL IS BASED ON THE IDEA THAT A SUCCESSFUL business concept, once proven, can be replicated across different locations by independent operators. Instead of the franchisor bearing the burden and risk of opening new locations on its own, it sells the rights to operate those locations to franchisees. In return, the franchisees get access to the franchisor's business model, products or services, and brand recognition, while also benefiting from training and support.

There are two main types of franchising: **product/trade name franchising** and **business format franchising**.

1 PRODUCT/TRADE NAME FRANCHISING: IN THIS MODEL, THE franchisee is primarily granted the right to sell a franchisor's products. The franchisee may operate an independent business but agrees to use the franchisor's trademark, brand, and perhaps certain operating methods. Examples of this model include automobile dealerships and soft drink bottlers.

2 BUSINESS FORMAT FRANCHISING: THIS IS THE MORE COMMON TYPE OF franchising, where the franchisee not only gets the right to use the franchisor's trademark and sell its products or services but also gains access to an entire business system. This includes everything from training, marketing, and operational procedures to sourcing supplies and managing customer service. Well-known examples include fast-food chains like McDonald's, retail outlets like 7-Eleven, and service providers like Merry Maids.

In business format franchising, the franchisor provides a detailed framework that the franchisee must follow to ensure consistency across all franchise locations. This standardization is crucial to maintaining the brand's integrity and reputation, as customers expect the same experience regardless of which location they visit.

. . .

FRANCHISOR VS. FRANCHISEE: ROLES AND RESPONSIBILITIES

Understanding the distinct roles and responsibilities of the franchisor and franchisee is key to operating within the franchise model. While franchising can be a rewarding business opportunity, it's essential to know where each party's duties begin and end.

Franchisor's Role:

The franchisor is the entity that created the business model and owns the brand. Its primary responsibility is to provide franchisees with the tools and support they need to run a successful operation. This can include:

• **Brand and Trademark:** The franchisor owns the brand, which is often the most valuable asset in a franchise system. Franchisees are granted the right to use the brand in their operations, which includes logos, slogans, and marketing materials.

• **Operating System:** The franchisor provides the franchisee with a comprehensive business system, including standard operating procedures (SOPs), employee training programs, and other systems designed to ensure consistent quality and service across all franchise locations.

• **Initial Training and Ongoing Support:** One of the key benefits of franchising is the training that franchisees receive from the franchisor. This typically includes an initial training program covering day-to-day operations, product knowledge, and customer service, as well as ongoing support in areas like marketing, accounting, and human resources.

• **Marketing and Advertising:** The franchisor often coordinates national or regional marketing campaigns that benefit the entire franchise network. Franchisees may also be required to contribute to local marketing efforts, but the franchisor generally takes the lead on larger-scale advertising.

• **Research and Development:** The franchisor is responsible for developing new products or services, improving business processes, and staying ahead of industry trends. Franchisees benefit from the franchisor's innovation without having to invest in research and development themselves.

Franchisee's Role:

The franchisee, on the other hand, is an independent business owner who enters into a contract with the franchisor to operate a business according to the franchisor's system. The franchisee invests capital to open and run the business, but they must adhere to the franchisor's guidelines. A franchisee's responsibilities typically include:

• **Initial Investment:** The franchisee is responsible for providing the necessary capital to open the business. This can include the franchise fee, startup costs (such as leasing or purchasing property, buying equipment, and hiring staff), and ongoing operating expenses.

• **Royalty Payments:** In most franchise systems, the franchisee is required to pay ongoing royalty fees to the franchisor, which are typically calculated as a percentage of the franchisee's gross sales. These payments compensate the franchisor for providing the business model, brand, and ongoing support.

• **Local Operations:** The franchisee is responsible for managing the day-to-day operations of the business. This includes hiring and training employees, overseeing customer service, managing finances, and ensuring that the franchise complies with both the franchisor's standards and local laws.

• **Adherence to Standards:** Franchisees must follow the franchisor's system to the letter. This includes everything from how products are made and delivered to how customer complaints are handled. Deviation from the system can result in penalties, termination of the franchise agreement, or legal action.

• **Local Marketing:** While the franchisor may handle large-scale advertising campaigns, the franchisee is often required to engage in local marketing efforts. This can include participating in community events, local media advertising, and social media campaigns specific to the franchisee's location.

·　·　·

The Benefits of Franchising

For many aspiring entrepreneurs, franchising offers a unique combination of support, structure, and independence. Below are some of the key benefits of buying into a franchise:

1 BRAND RECOGNITION: One of the most significant advantages of buying a franchise is instant brand recognition. Customers are more likely to trust an established brand with a proven track record than an unknown, untested business. For franchisees, this means starting with an existing customer base, rather than building one from the ground up.

2 PROVEN BUSINESS MODEL: Franchisees benefit from a business model that has already been tested and refined by the franchisor. This reduces much of the risk associated with starting a new business, as the franchisor has already identified what works and what doesn't.

3 TRAINING AND SUPPORT: Most franchisors offer extensive training and ongoing support to help franchisees succeed. Whether it's learning how to manage daily operations, troubleshooting customer service issues, or handling finances, franchisees have a built-in support system to guide them through the process.

4 MARKETING ASSISTANCE: Franchisors often manage large-scale marketing campaigns that benefit all franchise locations. This means franchisees can take advantage of national or regional advertising efforts without having to bear the full cost or responsibility.

· · ·

5 ECONOMIES OF SCALE: FRANCHISEES CAN OFTEN BENEFIT FROM THE franchisor's purchasing power, gaining access to goods and services at a lower cost than they would be able to negotiate on their own. This is especially beneficial for smaller franchisees who might not have the same leverage with suppliers as larger businesses.

6 REDUCED RISK: STARTING A BUSINESS IS ALWAYS A RISK, BUT franchising offers a lower-risk option compared to starting an independent business from scratch. The success of the franchise system provides a roadmap for the franchisee, reducing uncertainty and increasing the chances of success.

THE CHALLENGES OF FRANCHISING

While franchising has many benefits, it's not without its challenges. Prospective franchisees must be aware of the potential pitfalls that come with this business model:

1 LACK OF FLEXIBILITY: ONE OF THE BIGGEST DOWNSIDES OF franchising is the lack of flexibility. Franchisees are required to follow the franchisor's system and cannot make significant changes to the way the business operates. For entrepreneurs who enjoy creativity and independence, this can be frustrating.

2 ONGOING FEES: FRANCHISEES MUST PAY ONGOING ROYALTY FEES AND possibly marketing fees, which can eat into their profits. These fees are typically calculated as a percentage of gross sales, meaning that even if the franchisee is not making a significant profit, they are still obligated to make payments to the franchisor.

· · ·

3 TERRITORY RESTRICTIONS: MANY FRANCHISE AGREEMENTS INCLUDE territory restrictions, which can limit a franchisee's ability to expand or open additional locations within a desired area. While these restrictions are meant to protect the franchisee from competition within the brand, they can also limit growth opportunities. If a franchisee identifies a promising market just outside their designated territory, they may not have the option to pursue it, even if there is a high demand.

4 DEPENDENCE ON THE FRANCHISOR: FRANCHISEES RELY HEAVILY ON the franchisor for operational guidance, marketing support, and supply chain management. If the franchisor's performance falters, the franchisee's business can suffer as a result. In cases where franchisors experience financial difficulties or make poor business decisions, franchisees may find themselves in a precarious position with limited options to pivot or adapt.

5 BRAND REPUTATION RISKS: A FRANCHISEE'S SUCCESS IS CLOSELY TIED to the franchisor's brand image. If the brand as a whole suffers from negative publicity or if other franchisees fail to uphold quality standards, it can impact all locations, regardless of how well individual franchisees are performing. Maintaining a positive reputation is largely outside the Franchisee's control, which can make this a considerable risk.

6 LIMITED EXIT STRATEGIES: EXITING A FRANCHISE CAN BE MORE complex than selling an independent business. Franchise agreements often include strict conditions for transfer or sale, and the franchisor usually has the final say on whether a potential buyer can take over the business. This can limit a franchisee's ability to sell on favorable terms or at the right time.

Conclusion

In understanding the franchise business model, it becomes clear that franchising offers a unique blend of independence and support. The model allows individuals to operate their own business while benefiting from the established reputation, systems, and resources of a larger organization. This symbiotic relationship provides franchisors with expansion opportunities and franchisees with the guidance and structure needed to mitigate risks often associated with starting a business from scratch.

However, potential franchisees must approach this opportunity with a comprehensive understanding of the commitments, financial obligations, and operational expectations required. It is crucial to conduct thorough research, evaluate the franchise disclosure document (FDD) carefully, and consult with legal and financial professionals to ensure alignment with long-term goals.

The initial steps of entering a franchise system—whether it involves understanding the franchise agreement, assessing territory rights, or reviewing training and support—lay the groundwork for success. By fully grasping these foundational elements, franchisees position themselves to not only manage but also grow within their chosen system.

Ultimately, the franchise model is not a one-size-fits-all solution; it requires careful consideration, a strong work ethic, and a commitment to upholding the franchisor's brand standards. But for those who approach it with diligence and a strategic mindset, franchising offers a powerful vehicle for entrepreneurial success. In the next chapter, we will explore in greater depth the financial planning and operational strategies critical to thriving within a franchise system.

2

THE FRANCHISE DISCLOSURE DOCUMENT (FDD): YOUR FIRST LOOK

When stepping into the world of franchising, one of the most critical documents you will encounter is the Franchise Disclosure Document (FDD). It is your window into the franchise system you're considering, a legally mandated guide filled with vital information about the franchisor, the franchise model, and your responsibilities as a prospective franchisee. The FDD is regulated by the Federal Trade Commission (FTC) in the United States and is designed to protect potential franchisees by providing full transparency about the franchisor and its operations. Understanding how to navigate the FDD is a key part of the initial steps in the franchise process, and this chapter will give you a comprehensive overview of its importance and structure.

What Is the FDD?

The FDD serves as a cornerstone in the franchisor-franchisee relationship, offering essential disclosures about the franchise opportunity. Its primary purpose is to help potential franchisees make an informed decision before entering into a legally binding franchise agreement. The FDD outlines critical aspects of the franchise, including the franchisor's history, financial performance, litigation history, and the franchisee's obligations. It also provides detailed explanations of fees, operational support, marketing strategies, and other essential franchise systems.

By law, franchisors must provide the FDD to a prospective franchisee at least 14 days before any agreements are signed or fees are paid. This period allows potential franchisees the necessary time to review the document thoroughly and seek legal and financial advice before making a decision.

The Structure of the FDD: Key Items to Know

The FDD is structured into 23 distinct sections or "Items." Each of these items covers a different aspect of the franchise and is designed to provide full transparency on what you can expect as a franchisee. Let's take a closer look at some of the most crucial items within the FDD:

Item 1: The Franchisor and Any Parents, Predecessors, and Affiliates

This section provides an overview of the franchisor's business, its corporate history, and its relationship with any parent or affiliate companies. It offers insight into how long the franchisor has been in business, what services it provides, and its overall experience in the industry.

Item 3: Litigation

This item discloses any past or pending legal actions involving the franchisor. It's essential to understand whether the franchisor has been involved in disputes with other franchisees or third parties, as this could indicate potential red flags.

Item 5: Initial Fees

Item 5 details the upfront costs of joining the franchise, including the initial franchise fee and any other mandatory payments. This section is crucial for understanding your initial financial obligations.

Item 6: Other Fees

In addition to the initial fees, Item 6 provides a breakdown of ongoing fees, such as royalty payments, technology fees, marketing contributions, and more. Understanding these costs will help you gauge the total financial commitment over time.

Item 7: Estimated Initial Investment

This section outlines the range of financial investment required to open the franchise. It includes expenses such as equipment purchases, real estate costs, insurance, and other startup fees.

Item 12: Territory

Item 12 defines the geographical territory you will be granted as a franchisee and discusses whether you'll have exclusive rights to operate in that area. It also explains any restrictions on operating outside your territory, which could impact your growth and market reach.

Item 19: Financial Performance Representations

Item 19 provides information on the franchisor's financial performance, either through historical data or projections. Not all franchisors include this data, so it is critical to note whether financial performance representations are offered.

Item 21: Financial Statements

Item 21 includes the franchisor's audited financial statements, providing insights into the company's financial health. A stable franchisor with strong financials is often more likely to support its franchisees effectively over the long term.

How to Read and Interpret the FDD

Reading through the FDD can be overwhelming, particularly because of the technical legal and financial language. However, there are several strategies you can use to approach it effectively.

1. Focus on Key Items First

While all items in the FDD are important, it can help to prioritize certain sections that will have the most direct impact on your decision, such as the financial information (Items 5, 6, 7, 19, and 21) and territory (Item 12).

2. Work with Professionals

Engaging a franchise attorney and an accountant with franchising experience is highly recommended. These professionals can help you interpret complex language and provide guidance on what to look for in terms of risk and opportunity.

3. Compare Multiple FDDs

If you are considering multiple franchise opportunities, reviewing and comparing the FDDs side-by-side can provide valuable insights into how each franchisor operates and what they offer in terms of support, growth potential, and financial obligations.

4. Ask Questions

The FDD should provide answers to many of your questions, but it may also raise new ones. Don't hesitate to ask the franchisor for clarification on any points that are unclear or concerning. A transparent and responsive franchisor will be more than willing to address your concerns.

Red Flags in the FDD

While the FDD is designed to be transparent, not all franchise opportunities are created equal. Here are some potential red flags to watch for:

- **Excessive Litigation in Item 3:** If the franchisor has a history of legal disputes with franchisees, it may indicate problems with the system.
- **High Turnover Rates:** High numbers of terminated or transferred franchises may suggest dissatisfaction among franchisees.
- **Weak Financials in Item 21:** A franchisor with unstable or declining financial performance may not have the resources to support its franchisees effectively.
- **Unrealistic Financial Representations in Item 19:** If the franchisor provides financial projections that seem too good to be true, it's important to question the validity of those numbers.

The FDD as a Tool for Success

Ultimately, the FDD is a tool designed to empower you, the franchisee. It provides a clear view of the business model, its requirements, and potential risks and rewards. By taking the time to thoroughly review and understand the FDD, you position yourself to make an informed, confident decision about your future as a franchisee.

3

———

CHOOSING THE RIGHT FRANCHISE

Choosing the right franchise is one of the most critical decisions you will make as a potential business owner. With thousands of franchise systems available across various industries, selecting the right opportunity can seem overwhelming. However, by considering key factors such as personal goals, financial capacity, market conditions, and the support structure of the franchise, you can narrow your choices and find the right fit. In this chapter, we'll guide you through the process of choosing the best franchise for your unique situation, from initial research to making the final decision.

1. UNDERSTANDING YOUR GOALS AND MOTIVATIONS

Before diving into the specifics of various franchise systems, take a step back to reflect on your personal and professional goals. Why do you want to own a franchise, and what are you hoping to achieve?

Personal Goals

• **Lifestyle Considerations:** What kind of work-life balance are you looking for? Some franchises, like fast-food chains, require long hours, including weekends and holidays, while others may offer more flexibility.

• **Passion and Interests:** Are you passionate about the industry in which you're considering franchising? Operating a business you're interested in can have a significant impact on your long-term success and satisfaction.

• **Location Preferences:** Do you want a business that operates from a brick-and-mortar location, or would you prefer a home-based model? Where do you see yourself establishing your franchise—locally or in another region?

Professional Goals

• **Entrepreneurial Drive:** Do you want to take on a hands-on leadership role, or are you looking for a more passive investment?

• **Growth Aspirations:** Are you looking for a single franchise location, or do you envision expanding and operating multiple units over time?

• **Exit Strategy:** How long do you plan to own and operate the franchise? Is this a long-term venture, or do you see it as a stepping stone to other opportunities?

Understanding your personal and professional aspirations will provide a strong foundation as you begin evaluating different franchises.

2. Researching Franchise Opportunities

Once you have a clear understanding of your goals, the next step is to start researching franchise opportunities. This process requires time, attention to detail, and a methodical approach.

Identifying Industries of Interest

Start by exploring industries that align with your personal interests and market trends. Some of the most popular franchise sectors include:

• **Food and Beverage:** Fast food, casual dining, coffee shops, and ice cream parlors.

- **Retail:** Convenience stores, health and wellness products, apparel, and specialty items.
- **Home Services:** Cleaning, landscaping, home maintenance, and repair services.
- **Health and Fitness:** Gyms, fitness studios, personal training services, and health-related products.
- **Education and Childcare:** Tutoring centers, daycare facilities, and after-school programs.
- **Professional Services:** Accounting, legal services, business consulting, and marketing.

Look for industries that are growing, have long-term stability, and resonate with your passions and skills. Once you've identified potential industries, start researching specific franchise brands within those sectors.

Analyzing Franchise Performance

It's important to look beyond brand recognition and advertising appeal. Here are a few key indicators to consider when evaluating a franchise system:

- **Brand Strength:** How well-known is the brand, and does it have a positive reputation in the market? Established brands may offer greater support, but newer brands could present unique growth opportunities.
- **Franchise Success Rates:** How many franchisees are succeeding within the system? Investigate turnover rates and whether existing franchisees are satisfied with their business performance.
- **Market Demand:** Is there a growing demand for the franchise's products or services in your area? Conducting local market research can help determine whether the franchise concept will be viable in your location.

The FDD and Financial Health

The Franchise Disclosure Document (FDD), which we discussed in detail in the previous chapter, plays a key role in understanding the financial aspects of a franchise. Pay close attention to the financial health of the franchisor, including Items 5, 6, and 7, which detail initial fees, ongoing costs, and the estimated total investment required.

3. EVALUATING FRANCHISE SUPPORT SYSTEMS

One of the most valuable aspects of owning a franchise is the built-in support network. However, the level of support provided can vary greatly from one franchisor to another. Assessing the strength of a franchise's support structure is crucial when making your decision.

Initial Training

A comprehensive training program can make all the difference in your ability to successfully launch your franchise. Consider the following questions:

- How extensive is the initial training program?
- Does it cover both operational and managerial aspects of running the business?
- Will you have access to hands-on training at an existing franchise location?

Ongoing Support

Strong franchisors provide ongoing support to ensure the continued success of their franchisees. This may include:

- **Field Support:** Do you have access to a dedicated field representative who can assist with operations, marketing, and business growth?
- **Marketing Assistance:** What kind of marketing support does the franchisor provide? This could include national advertising campaigns, local marketing strategies, and social media support.
- **Technology and Systems:** Does the franchise offer technology solutions for managing inventory, payroll, scheduling, and customer relations?

Franchisee Community

The strength of the franchisee network is another important consideration. A supportive franchisee community allows you to share best practices, troubleshoot problems, and build relationships with other franchisees. Look for franchisors that foster a collaborative and open environment among their franchisees.

4. UNDERSTANDING YOUR FINANCIAL COMMITMENT

Choosing a franchise is not only a business decision but a financial one. It's essential to have a clear understanding of the total cost of ownership and the potential return on investment.

Initial Investment

The initial franchise fee is just one part of the financial equation. You'll also need to consider:

- **Build-out Costs:** This includes real estate, construction, and equipment purchases for your franchise location.

- **Working Capital:** You'll need sufficient cash reserves to cover operating expenses during the early months of operation, which can vary depending on the type of franchise.

- **Marketing Funds:** Some franchisors require you to contribute to a national marketing fund, and you may also need to allocate funds for local marketing efforts.

Ongoing Costs

In addition to the initial investment, ongoing costs such as royalties, advertising fees, and technology fees must be factored into your business plan. Make sure you fully understand the financial commitments outlined in the FDD.

Financing Options

Depending on your financial situation, you may need to explore various financing options to fund your franchise. Common sources of financing include:

- **Small Business Loans (SBA):** Many franchise systems qualify for SBA loans, which offer favorable terms and lower interest rates.

- **Franchisor Financing:** Some franchisors offer in-house financing or partnerships with third-party lenders.

- **Personal Funds:** Using personal savings or equity from other assets can also be a viable option, but be sure to assess the risks.

5. Making the Final Decision

After conducting thorough research, evaluating potential franchises, and understanding your financial responsibilities, you're ready to make the final decision. This is not a decision to take lightly, so take time to reflect and consult with key advisors, such as a franchise attorney, accountant, and business mentor.

Ask the Right Questions

- Do I believe in the franchise's business model and value proposition?
- Does this franchise align with my personal and professional goals?
- Am I comfortable with the financial risks and rewards of this investment?
- Do I feel confident in the franchisor's ability to provide the support I need for success?

Consult Existing Franchisees

Speaking with current franchisees can provide valuable insights into the real-world experience of owning the franchise. Ask them about their experience with the franchisor's support, their financial performance, and whether they would make the same decision again.

Conclusion

Choosing the right franchise is a process that requires careful thought, research, and planning. By understanding your personal motivations, researching various opportunities, evaluating support systems, and assessing your financial capabilities, you can position yourself for success as a franchisee. The right franchise will not only meet your business goals but will also provide a fulfilling and rewarding career path.

PART II

THE FRANCHISE AGREEMENT

4

DISSECTING THE FRANCHISE AGREEMENT

Entering into a franchise agreement is one of the most significant legal steps an entrepreneur will take when purchasing a franchise. While the Franchise Disclosure Document (FDD) gives you a comprehensive overview of the franchise system, the franchise agreement is where the legal obligations between the franchisor and franchisee are formalized. Every clause, term, and condition within this document will affect the way you operate your business and the relationship you will have with the franchisor for the duration of the franchise term.

Because the franchise agreement is a legally binding contract, it's essential to understand its contents before signing. This chapter will dissect the franchise agreement, helping you understand its key components, common legal terms, potential pitfalls, and the role of legal counsel in negotiating terms that align with your business goals.

What Is a Franchise Agreement?

At its core, the franchise agreement is the formal legal contract that binds the franchisor and franchisee. It grants the franchisee the right to operate a business under the franchisor's brand, using the franchisor's systems, trademarks, and intellectual property. In exchange, the franchisee agrees to adhere to specific operational standards, pay required fees, and follow guidelines set by the franchisor.

The agreement serves several functions:

- **Defines the relationship** between the franchisor and franchisee.
- **Details the obligations** of both parties.
- **Establishes the franchisee's rights** to use the franchisor's intellectual property and operating systems.
- **Protects the franchisor's brand** and proprietary information.
- **Clarifies the financial commitments** of the franchisee, including initial and ongoing fees.

Franchise agreements are typically non-negotiable, at least in their broader structure, because franchisors need consistency across their franchise network. However, certain provisions—particularly those relating to territory, fees, or specific operational terms—may sometimes be subject to negotiation. This is where a franchise attorney can be invaluable.

Key Components of the Franchise Agreement

Understanding the primary sections of a franchise agreement is critical to making an informed decision. While each franchise agreement may vary slightly depending on the brand or industry, most agreements contain similar core elements. Below is a breakdown of the key components that you should carefully review:

1. GRANT OF FRANCHISE AND TERM

THE GRANT OF FRANCHISE SECTION OUTLINES WHAT RIGHTS THE franchisee is being granted. This includes the right to use the franchisor's trademarks, trade name, and operating system. It will also specify any limitations on these rights. For example, the agreement may grant you the right to use the franchisor's brand only within a certain geographic region or for a certain period of time.

The **Term** specifies the length of time the agreement will last. Most franchise agreements have terms ranging from five to twenty years, depending on the industry. Pay close attention to the length of the term and any renewal options. Franchise agreements generally provide for renewals, but these renewals may require signing a new agreement with different terms or paying additional fees.

2. TERRITORY

ONE OF THE MOST CRITICAL ASPECTS OF ANY FRANCHISE AGREEMENT IS the **Territory** clause, which defines the area in which you have the right to operate your franchise. Territories can either be **exclusive** or **non-exclusive.** In an exclusive territory, the franchisor agrees not to open or allow another franchisee to operate within your designated area. In a non-exclusive territory, you may face direct competition from other franchisees or even company-owned locations within your geographic area.

Pay particular attention to any conditions under which the franchisor can alter your territory. For example, some agreements allow franchisors to shrink a territory if certain performance metrics are not met. Additionally, you should check if you're allowed to market outside of your territory or serve customers from other areas, as these conditions can significantly affect your potential revenue.

3. FRANCHISE FEES AND OTHER PAYMENTS

THE FRANCHISE FEE SECTION WILL DETAIL THE FINANCIAL OBLIGATIONS of the franchisee. These typically include:

• **Initial Franchise Fee:** The one-time fee paid upfront to join the franchise. This fee is generally non-refundable and covers the cost of entry into the franchise system, including initial training, support, and the right to use the franchisor's brand.

• **Royalties:** The ongoing payments that franchisees make to the franchisor, usually based on a percentage of gross sales. Royalties can range from 4% to 12%, depending on the franchise. Be sure to understand how royalties are calculated—whether they're based on gross or net sales—and whether there are minimum monthly royalties regardless of performance.

• **Marketing Fees:** Most franchisors charge a national or regional marketing fee, which funds advertising campaigns for the brand. This is typically an additional percentage of your revenue, often around 1% to 4%. Be sure to review what control you have over local advertising and marketing initiatives, as well as what support the franchisor provides.

• **Technology Fees:** In today's market, many franchisors charge technology or software fees to maintain point-of-sale systems, websites, or apps. These fees should be clearly defined in the agreement.

Additionally, be aware of **additional fees** that might be charged for training, support, equipment purchases, or territory expansion.

4. Franchisor Obligations

THE FRANCHISE AGREEMENT WILL OUTLINE THE SPECIFIC OBLIGATIONS OF the franchisor. These typically include providing:

• **Initial Training:** Most franchisors offer comprehensive initial training for new franchisees and their staff. This training covers everything from daily operations to financial management, marketing, and customer service.

• **Ongoing Support:** The agreement should detail the level of ongoing support provided by the franchisor. This can include field support representatives, marketing resources, and regular operational reviews.

- **Marketing and Advertising:** While the franchisee may contribute to a national or regional marketing fund, the franchisor is usually responsible for managing larger advertising campaigns.
- **Approved Suppliers:** The franchisor may also provide a list of approved suppliers or products that you are required to use to ensure brand consistency across all locations.

A key aspect to note is that while franchisors are required to provide support, they often reserve the right to alter or reduce their services. Make sure you understand the extent of the support being offered and whether the franchisor has any obligations to increase their level of involvement if challenges arise.

5. Franchisee Obligations

This section will outline your obligations as a franchisee. These obligations can be extensive and will dictate how you must operate your business. Key responsibilities may include:

- **Operational Standards:** Franchisees are required to follow the franchisor's operational guidelines, which can cover everything from the layout of your store to customer service protocols, marketing materials, and pricing strategies. Deviation from these standards can result in penalties or even termination.
- **Training Requirements:** Beyond the initial training, franchisees are often required to attend ongoing training sessions or provide training to their staff. Ensure you understand the time and cost involved in meeting these training obligations.
- **Reporting Requirements:** Franchise agreements typically require franchisees to provide regular reports on financial performance, inventory, and other key operational metrics. This allows the franchisor to monitor the health of the franchise network.
- **Adherence to Intellectual Property Rules:** Franchisees must strictly adhere to guidelines for using the franchisor's trademarks,

logos, and intellectual property. Any misuse of the brand could result in legal action.

Franchisee obligations are typically non-negotiable, and franchisors will enforce them to maintain consistency across their brand.

6. Renewal and Termination

The Renewal and Termination clauses dictate what happens when the franchise term ends or if either party wishes to end the agreement prematurely.

- **Renewal:** Review the renewal terms carefully. Some franchisors require franchisees to meet certain performance benchmarks or make additional investments to qualify for renewal. Others may require signing an entirely new agreement, which may have updated terms that could be less favorable.

- **Termination:** This clause outlines the grounds for terminating the franchise agreement. Franchisors typically reserve the right to terminate the agreement for reasons such as:
  - Failure to pay royalties or other fees.
  - Violation of operational standards.
  - Bankruptcy or insolvency.
  - Criminal behavior or fraudulent activity.

The franchisee may also have the right to terminate, but often with significant financial penalties. Review the termination clause to understand the conditions under which either party can walk away and what financial obligations (such as liquidated damages) remain upon termination.

7. Transfer of Ownership

. . .

IF YOU EVER WANT TO SELL YOUR FRANCHISE, THE **TRANSFER OF Ownership** section will govern the process. Franchisors typically have strict rules regarding transfers, often requiring:

- Prior written consent from the franchisor.
- Payment of a transfer fee.
- The new owner to meet the franchisor's approval criteria and undergo training.

Ensure you understand these provisions, as they may affect your ability to sell your franchise if you decide to exit the business.

8. NON-COMPETE AND CONFIDENTIALITY CLAUSES

MOST FRANCHISE AGREEMENTS INCLUDE **NON-COMPETE AND Confidentiality Clauses** designed to protect the franchisor's proprietary information and prevent franchisees from competing with the brand during and after the franchise term.

- **Non-Compete Clause:** This clause restricts franchisees from owning or operating a similar business that competes with the franchise, both during the term and for a certain period after the agreement ends. Review the geographic scope and duration of the non-compete clause to ensure it is reasonable and does not overly restrict your future business opportunities.
- **Confidentiality Clause:** Franchisees are often required to sign a confidentiality agreement prohibiting them from disclosing trade secrets or proprietary information learned during the franchise relationship during the franchise relationship. This can include things like business processes, marketing strategies, vendor relationships, and operational manuals. The confidentiality clause typically remains in effect even after the franchise agreement has been terminated or expired. Failing to adhere to these clauses can result in legal action.

. . .

9. Dispute Resolution

While every franchise relationship aims to be mutually beneficial, disputes can and do arise. The **Dispute Resolution** section outlines the procedures for resolving disagreements between the franchisor and franchisee. This section can include several mechanisms for resolving conflicts:

• **Mediation:** Some franchise agreements require mediation as a first step. In mediation, both parties attempt to reach a mutually acceptable solution with the help of a neutral third party. It's usually a quicker and less expensive process than litigation.

• **Arbitration:** Many franchise agreements require arbitration rather than court litigation. Arbitration is a private process where an arbitrator (or panel of arbitrators) hears both sides and makes a binding decision. While arbitration is often seen as more efficient than going to court, franchisees should understand that the outcome is typically final and cannot be appealed.

• **Jurisdiction and Venue:** Franchise agreements will often specify where disputes must be resolved—usually in the franchisor's home state. This can pose logistical challenges for franchisees located far from the franchisor's headquarters, and it's something you should factor in when considering potential disputes.

It's important to review this section carefully, as the methods for resolving disputes and the location of resolution can significantly affect both the cost and ease of resolving a disagreement.

10. Franchisor's Right to Modify the Agreement

In some agreements, the franchisor reserves the right to modify certain terms of the franchise relationship over time. For example, they may reserve the right to adjust operating standards, introduce new products or services, or revise marketing strategies. While flexibility can be beneficial for adapting to market trends, it also means that the franchisor could impose changes that significantly affect your business operations.

Look carefully at this clause to understand the extent of the franchisor's control over future modifications and whether you have any input or recourse if changes are made that negatively impact your business.

Potential Pitfalls in Franchise Agreements

Even with careful review, there are several common pitfalls that franchisees may encounter when entering into a franchise agreement. Being aware of these can help you avoid costly mistakes:

- **Underestimating Fees:** Many franchisees focus primarily on the initial franchise fee and royalties, but ongoing costs like marketing fees, technology fees, and renewal fees can quickly add up. Be sure to calculate the full cost of owning and operating the franchise over time.

- **Vague Support Obligations:** Some franchise agreements include vague promises of support from the franchisor. If the level of support is not clearly defined, you may find yourself receiving less assistance than you anticipated. Be sure to ask for specifics regarding the nature and frequency of ongoing support.

- **Performance Expectations:** Some agreements may include minimum performance requirements that can be difficult to meet, especially in the early years of operation. If you fail to meet these benchmarks, your franchise territory or contract could be at risk. Ensure that these expectations are reasonable and aligned with your market conditions.

- **Non-Compete Clauses:** Non-compete clauses that are overly broad or long-lasting can severely restrict your ability to operate other businesses in the same or related industries. Before signing, make sure the non-compete clause is narrowly tailored to the scope of the business and the region in which you operate.

- **Limited Exit Strategies:** Selling a franchise can be more difficult than anticipated, especially if the franchisor retains strict control over the transfer process. Make sure you understand the conditions and fees involved if you ever want to exit the franchise.

The Role of a Franchise Attorney

Given the complexity of franchise agreements and the potential for long-term legal and financial implications, it is highly advisable to work with a franchise attorney before signing. A franchise attorney can:

• **Provide Expert Analysis:** An experienced attorney can review the entire franchise agreement, ensuring that you fully understand each clause and how it will impact your business. They can identify any potential red flags and advise you on areas where you may want to negotiate.

• **Negotiate Key Terms:** While many parts of a franchise agreement are non-negotiable, certain areas (like territory, fees, or performance obligations) may offer room for negotiation. A franchise attorney can help advocate on your behalf to secure more favorable terms.

• **Ensure Compliance with Legal Standards:** Franchise agreements must comply with federal and state franchise laws, such as the Federal Trade Commission's (FTC) Franchise Rule and various state regulations. An attorney will ensure that the agreement is in compliance with these laws and that your rights are protected.

• **Assist in Dispute Resolution:** If disputes arise during the course of your franchise relationship, your attorney can help guide you through the mediation or arbitration process, or represent you in court if necessary.

FINAL THOUGHTS: PROTECTING YOUR INVESTMENT

Signing a franchise agreement is a major step in your entrepreneurial journey, but it's also a significant financial and legal commitment. This document will govern your relationship with the franchisor for many years, so it's critical to ensure that you fully understand its contents and implications. By carefully reviewing the agreement, asking the right questions, and working with a knowledgeable franchise attorney, you can protect your investment and set your business up for long-term success.

Always remember that entering a franchise system is not just about buying into a brand—it's about forging a long-term partnership with the franchisor. The terms of the franchise agreement will shape that partnership and the success of your franchise. Take the time to thoroughly dissect the agreement before signing, and approach the process with the due diligence it deserves.

5

NEGOTIATING THE FRANCHISE AGREEMENT

Franchise agreements are often presented as "non-negotiable," especially by larger, more established franchise systems. Franchisors typically offer a standardized agreement to maintain consistency across their franchise network and to protect their brand. However, in certain cases, some terms may be negotiable, particularly with smaller or emerging franchise systems that are looking to expand. Even with larger franchises, there are sometimes limited opportunities to negotiate specific provisions.

The key to negotiating a franchise agreement is understanding what is reasonable to request, identifying areas where you can ask for concessions, and knowing when to push for changes. In this chapter, we will delve into the negotiation process, outline which terms may be open to discussion, and provide strategies for successfully negotiating more favorable terms in your franchise agreement. While it's important to enter negotiations with clear objectives, it's equally important to approach the process with realistic expectations.

I. UNDERSTANDING THE FRANCHISOR'S PERSPECTIVE

Before entering into negotiations, it's crucial to understand why franchisors typically resist making changes to their standard franchise agreement. For a franchisor, consistency across their franchise network is paramount. Offering different terms to different franchisees can lead to confusion, operational inconsistencies, and even legal complications. Franchisors also have a vested interest in protecting their brand and ensuring that all franchisees follow the same guidelines and operational procedures.

Additionally, many large franchisors have invested significant time and resources into drafting franchise agreements that are legally sound and enforceable across various jurisdictions. Making changes to the agreement for one franchisee could open the door for others to demand similar concessions, creating administrative and operational challenges for the franchisor.

However, franchisors also recognize the importance of growth and expansion. Smaller or emerging franchisors, in particular, may be more flexible in their negotiations, especially if they are eager to attract quality franchisees to grow their brand.

2. IDENTIFYING NEGOTIABLE TERMS

While many terms in a franchise agreement may be set in stone, there are certain provisions that may be open to negotiation. It's important to approach the negotiation process with a clear understanding of which terms are more likely to be flexible and which are not.

Here are some key areas where franchisees may have room to negotiate:

A. Territory

The definition and exclusivity of the territory granted to the franchisee is often one of the most negotiable and critically important aspects of a franchise agreement. Territory rights can have a significant impact on the franchisee's ability to grow their business, avoid internal competition, and maximize profitability. A well-defined and sufficiently protected territory is essential for franchisees who want to ensure that they have the space to operate without interference from other franchisees or the franchisor's company-owned locations.

When negotiating the territory provision of a franchise agreement, franchisees should begin by seeking to clarify the exact boundaries of the territory they will be granted. This includes obtaining a detailed description of the geographical area, whether it's defined by zip codes, city limits, population metrics, or a specific radius around the franchisee's location. Ensuring there is no ambiguity in the territorial definition is key to avoiding future disputes or misunderstandings, which could otherwise lead to significant legal and operational complications.

Exclusivity is another critical element of territory negotiations. An exclusive territory means that the franchisee will have the sole right to operate within that specified area, and neither the franchisor nor other franchisees can establish competing businesses in the same market. If exclusivity is offered, the franchisee should seek clear and specific language in the agreement that prohibits not only other franchisees but also company-owned stores or even e-commerce operations from encroaching on the territory.

In situations where the franchisor offers a **non-exclusive** territory, franchisees should be particularly vigilant about potential threats to their business from nearby franchise locations or company-owned operations. Non-exclusive territories allow the franchisor to open other franchises or company-owned locations within close proximity, which could severely impact the franchisee's customer base. In these cases, it's worth negotiating additional protections or guarantees to mitigate the risk. For example, a franchisee may request a **buffer zone** around their location—an area of a specified radius where no other locations (franchised or company-owned) can be opened. This could give the franchisee a de facto form of exclusivity within a practical operating distance, even if the territory is technically classified as non-exclusive.

Another potential point of negotiation in non-exclusive territory arrangements is the **right of first refusal**. This clause gives the franchisee the option to open new locations within nearby areas before the franchisor offers them to other potential franchisees. If the franchisor identifies an opportunity to open a new franchise in a neighboring territory, the franchisee with the right of first refusal can choose whether they want to expand into that area before anyone else is given the chance. This can provide valuable growth opportunities for franchisees who are looking to build a multi-unit operation, while simultaneously protecting their existing business from immediate competition.

In addition to negotiating the boundaries and exclusivity of a territory, franchisees may also be able to secure the right to **expand their territory** or open additional units based on performance. Franchisors often include benchmarks related to sales performance, customer satisfaction, or operational compliance that, if met, could trigger the option for the franchisee to expand their territory or open new franchise locations. This kind of arrangement is mutually beneficial: it provides the franchisee with a clear growth trajectory while allowing the franchisor to reward successful franchisees with further opportunities.

For example, a franchisee who demonstrates strong sales growth and market penetration within their current territory may negotiate a clause that allows them to open additional units in nearby areas without facing competition from other franchisees. This ensures that as their business grows, they won't be restricted to their original boundaries, and they'll be able to capitalize on new market opportunities that arise organically from their success.

At the same time, the franchisee may want to ensure that the franchise agreement contains safeguards against **over-saturation** in a given market. Even with the right to open additional units, it's essential to ensure that the market can sustain multiple locations without cannibalizing sales. A territory that becomes over-saturated with too many locations (whether franchised or company-owned) can lead to diminishing returns for each unit, ultimately affecting the profitability and viability of the franchisee's business. Therefore, franchisees may negotiate limits on the number of units that can be opened within a certain geographic radius, or seek assurances from the franchisor that they will conduct market feasibility studies before approving new locations within close proximity.

In some cases, franchisees may also explore the possibility of negotiating **territorial protection for legacy clients** in the event that the franchisor later decides to carve up a previously unclaimed or unprotected area. For instance, if a franchisee has been servicing customers from outside their designated territory (due to a lack of nearby franchisees or the absence of territorial exclusivity), they may want to negotiate protections that allow them to retain those customers even if the franchisor later opens a new franchise location in that area. This kind of clause can be especially important in industries where long-term client relationships or ongoing service contracts are a core component of the business model.

Furthermore, franchisees should be aware that **territory provisions** can also be tied to the franchisee's own performance. In some cases, franchisors may retain the right to reduce or modify a franchisee's territory if they fail to meet certain performance standards or sales targets. This is why it's crucial to carefully review any performance-related conditions in the franchise agreement and negotiate for reasonable thresholds that account for market fluctuations, seasonality, or other external factors that could impact sales. Franchisees may also want to include provisions that allow for a grace period or performance improvement plan before any territorial adjustments are made.

Ultimately, the territory provision in a franchise agreement can be one of the most crucial factors in determining the franchisee's success. Securing a clearly defined, exclusive territory that offers room for growth can provide a solid foundation for building a thriving franchise business. Conversely, vague or poorly protected territories can expose franchisees to unnecessary risks and competitive threats. By carefully negotiating these provisions and seeking appropriate protections, franchisees can ensure that their territory rights align with their business goals and set themselves up for long-term success within the franchise system.

It's essential to approach territory negotiations with a thorough understanding of both the local market conditions and the specific dynamics of the franchise system. Consulting with a franchise attorney or business advisor who has experience in territory negotiations can provide valuable insights and help ensure that the final agreement includes the necessary safeguards to protect the franchisee's interests. Ultimately, securing the right territory terms can give franchisees the competitive edge they need to maximize their potential within the franchise system.

B. Marketing Fees

Most franchise agreements require franchisees to contribute to a national or regional advertising fund, usually through a set percentage of gross sales. While the percentage itself may be non-negotiable, franchisees can request more transparency regarding how the marketing funds are used and whether any portion of the funds will be allocated specifically to their local market. Franchisees may also be able to negotiate a waiver or reduction in marketing fees during the first year of operation to allow them to focus on local marketing efforts.

C. Training and Support

Training and ongoing support are critical components of a successful franchise, and these provisions are often included in the franchise agreement. However, the scope and quality of training can vary widely between franchisors. Franchisees should carefully review the training program outlined in the agreement and negotiate for additional training or extended support if they feel it's necessary. This is particularly important for franchisees who are new to the industry or have limited experience in the franchised business model.

D. Renewal and Termination Provisions

The terms of renewal and termination are often overlooked during the initial negotiation process, but they can have a significant impact on the franchisee's long-term success. Franchisees should carefully review the renewal provisions and negotiate for more favorable terms, such as the right to renew without additional fees or a reduction in royalty rates for renewal periods.

Termination provisions are equally important, as they dictate the circumstances under which the franchisor can terminate the agreement. Franchisees should seek to limit the franchisor's ability to terminate the agreement without cause and negotiate for a longer notice period in the event of a termination.

E. Transferability

If the franchisee decides to sell their business in the future, the transferability provisions in the franchise agreement will determine the process and conditions for transferring ownership. Franchisees should negotiate for the right to transfer the business to a qualified buyer with minimal interference from the franchisor. In some cases, franchisees may also be able to negotiate a waiver of transfer fees or the right to pass the business on to family members.

3. Strategies for Successful Negotiation

Negotiating a franchise agreement requires preparation, strategy, and clear communication. Here are some key strategies for achieving a successful outcome:

A. Do Your Homework

Before entering into negotiations, franchisees should thoroughly research the franchisor and the franchise system. This includes reviewing the Franchise Disclosure Document (FDD), speaking with current and former franchisees, and consulting with a franchise attorney. Understanding the franchisor's business model, financial health, and track record of franchisee support will provide valuable insights into the franchisor's priorities and potential areas for negotiation.

B. Prioritize Your Objectives

It's important to go into negotiations with a clear understanding of what is most important to you as a franchisee. While it may be tempting to ask for changes to multiple provisions, focusing on your top priorities will increase your chances of success. For example, if territorial exclusivity is critical to your business plan, prioritize that over less important terms like marketing fees. By focusing on your key objectives, you'll be able to make more targeted and persuasive arguments during negotiations.

C. Build a Strong Case

When negotiating with a franchisor, it's essential to build a strong case for why the requested changes are reasonable and in the best interest of both parties. This may involve providing data on local market conditions, demonstrating your business experience and expertise, or highlighting potential benefits to the franchisor, such as faster expansion or increased brand awareness in a new market.

D. Be Prepared to Compromise

Negotiation is a two-way street, and it's important to be prepared for compromise. While you may not get everything you ask for, being flexible and willing to find common ground can lead to a more favorable overall agreement. In some cases, you may be able to negotiate concessions in one area in exchange for agreeing to the franchisor's terms in another.

E. Get Everything in Writing

Any changes to the franchise agreement that are agreed upon during negotiations must be documented in writing. Verbal agreements are not legally binding, and any concessions or modifications to the standard agreement should be included in a formal addendum or amendment. It's essential to review the final agreement with your attorney to ensure that all negotiated terms are accurately reflected.

· · ·

4. WORKING WITH A FRANCHISE ATTORNEY

One of the most important steps in the negotiation process is working with an experienced franchise attorney. A franchise attorney can help you identify areas for negotiation, draft proposed changes to the agreement, and ensure that your interests are protected throughout the process. They can also provide valuable insights into industry standards and help you avoid common pitfalls that inexperienced franchisees may overlook.

5. CONCLUSION

Negotiating a franchise agreement can be a complex and challenging process, but with the right approach, it's possible to secure more favorable terms that support your business goals. By understanding the franchisor's perspective, identifying key areas for negotiation, and employing effective negotiation strategies, you can create a partnership that benefits both parties and sets the foundation for long-term success.

While some provisions in a franchise agreement may be non-negotiable, others can be tailored to your specific needs and circumstances. The key is to approach the process with preparation, professionalism, and a willingness to find common ground. With the right support from a qualified franchise attorney and a clear understanding of your priorities, you'll be well-equipped to negotiate a franchise agreement that positions you for success.

6

KEY LEGAL PITFALLS AND HOW TO AVOID THEM

When entering into a franchise agreement, it's essential to recognize that while franchising offers many advantages, it also carries specific legal risks. These risks, or legal pitfalls, can arise from misunderstanding contractual obligations, entering into a poorly structured agreement, or encountering unforeseen operational challenges. Failing to address these risks upfront can lead to costly legal disputes, financial losses, or, in the worst-case scenario, the termination of your franchise.

In this chapter, we'll discuss the most common legal pitfalls franchisees encounter and provide strategies for avoiding them. Whether you're new to franchising or have previous experience, understanding the legal landscape of franchising is crucial to safeguarding your investment and ensuring long-term success. Armed with this knowledge, you can navigate potential legal hazards with confidence and avoid pitfalls that might undermine your business.

1. FAILING TO UNDERSTAND THE FRANCHISE DISCLOSURE DOCUMENT (FDD)

One of the most important legal documents in the franchising process is the **Franchise Disclosure Document (FDD)**. This document is provided to prospective franchisees by the franchisor and contains critical information about the franchise system, the franchisor's background, and the terms of the franchise agreement. The FDD is designed to protect prospective franchisees by ensuring transparency and providing the information necessary to make an informed investment decision.

Pitfall: Many franchisees either fail to thoroughly review the FDD or do not fully understand the significance of the information it contains. Skimming through the FDD or rushing to sign the franchise agreement without seeking legal advice can result in franchisees overlooking key details about fees, territorial rights, training obligations, or dispute resolution mechanisms.

How to Avoid It: Take the time to read the FDD carefully, paying special attention to sections such as Item 5 (initial fees), Item 6 (other fees), Item 7 (estimated initial investment), Item 12 (territory), and Item 19 (financial performance representations). It is highly recommended that you work with a franchise attorney to interpret the FDD and identify any potential red flags. An attorney can help you ask the right questions and clarify anything that may be unclear, ensuring that you fully understand what you're agreeing to before signing the franchise agreement.

2. MISUNDERSTANDING OR OVERLOOKING KEY CONTRACTUAL TERMS

The franchise agreement is a legally binding contract that outlines the rights and obligations of both the franchisor and the franchisee. It is the cornerstone of your relationship with the franchisor and governs how you will operate your franchise business.

Pitfall: A common legal pitfall for franchisees is misunderstanding or overlooking key contractual terms. This can include provisions related to royalty payments, marketing fees, territorial restrictions, renewal rights, or termination clauses. Many franchisees are eager to move forward with their new business and may gloss over these details, only to face issues later when they realize they are locked into unfavorable terms.

How to Avoid It: Review the franchise agreement with a fine-tooth comb, ideally with the help of an experienced franchise attorney. Pay close attention to the following key provisions:

- **Royalty Payments and Fees:** Understand how royalties are calculated (typically as a percentage of gross sales) and when they are due. Ensure you are clear on any other fees, such as advertising contributions or technology fees.

- **Territorial Rights:** Clarify the boundaries of your territory and whether you have exclusive rights to operate within that area. Negotiate for more favorable terms if possible.

- **Renewal and Termination:** Understand the conditions under which the franchise agreement can be renewed or terminated. Make sure you are aware of the franchisor's ability to terminate the agreement and what constitutes a breach of contract.

- **Non-Compete Clauses:** Many franchise agreements include non-compete provisions that restrict the franchisee's ability to operate a similar business during or after the term of the agreement. Review these clauses carefully and assess their impact on your future business opportunities.

3. Underestimating the Importance of Territorial Protections

The territory provision in a franchise agreement defines the area in which the franchisee is allowed to operate and potentially limits the franchisor's ability to place other franchisees or company-owned locations within that area.

Pitfall: Franchisees often underestimate the importance of having well-defined and sufficiently protected territories. Without adequate territorial protection, franchisees may find themselves competing with other franchisees or company-owned stores in close proximity, leading to market saturation and reduced profits.

How to Avoid It: Ensure that your franchise agreement provides clear, enforceable territorial protections. If the agreement offers an exclusive territory, make sure the boundaries are clearly defined and that no other franchise locations or company-owned stores can be opened within that area. If the territory is non-exclusive, negotiate for additional protections, such as the right of first refusal for nearby territories or restrictions on the proximity of other locations. Carefully assess whether the territory you are granted has enough potential customers to sustain your business.

4. Ignoring or Misunderstanding Financial Obligations

Franchising comes with several financial obligations, some of which are ongoing throughout the life of the franchise. These obligations typically include initial fees, royalty payments, marketing contributions, and costs associated with purchasing inventory or services from the franchisor.

Pitfall: Franchisees sometimes fail to fully appreciate the extent of their financial commitments. This can lead to cash flow issues, unexpected expenses, or even defaulting on their contractual obligations. For example, a franchisee may not realize the financial burden of mandatory marketing fees or underestimate the long-term impact of royalty payments on profitability.

How to Avoid It: Review the financial obligations outlined in the FDD and franchise agreement in detail. Use Item 7 of the FDD, which provides an estimate of the initial investment, to create a comprehensive financial plan that takes into account all fees and expenses. Pay close attention to recurring fees, such as royalties and marketing contributions, and factor them into your long-term financial projections. Make sure you have adequate capital reserves to meet these obligations, especially during the initial phase of the business when revenues may be lower.

5. Inadequate Protection Against Franchisor Control

One of the primary benefits of franchising is the use of a proven business model and established brand. However, the franchisor retains significant control over how the franchisee operates their business, which can sometimes lead to conflicts or frustrations if the franchisee feels overly restricted.

Pitfall: Some franchisees fail to recognize the level of control the franchisor can exert over their day-to-day operations. This can include mandates on suppliers, pricing structures, marketing strategies, and even the appearance of the physical location. Franchisees who are not fully prepared for this level of control may find themselves in conflict with the franchisor or unable to make independent business decisions.

How to Avoid It: Before signing the franchise agreement, carefully review the franchisor's operational requirements and restrictions. Ensure that you are comfortable with the level of control the franchisor will have over your business. Pay particular attention to clauses related to approved suppliers, mandatory marketing programs, and pricing policies. If possible, negotiate for more flexibility in areas that are important to you, such as the ability to choose local suppliers or implement customized marketing strategies.

6. FAILURE TO PLAN FOR DISPUTE RESOLUTION

Even with the best intentions, disputes can arise between franchisors and franchisees. These disputes may relate to territorial rights, fee disputes, performance expectations, or breaches of contract. The way disputes are handled is typically outlined in the franchise agreement.

Pitfall: Some franchisees fail to adequately plan for how disputes will be resolved. This can result in costly and time-consuming litigation, which may damage the franchise relationship and drain financial resources.

How to Avoid It: Review the dispute resolution provisions in the franchise agreement carefully. Many franchise agreements include clauses that require disputes to be resolved through mediation or arbitration, rather than litigation. While these alternative dispute resolution methods can be faster and less expensive than going to court, it's important to understand the specific procedures outlined in the agreement. If the agreement includes a mandatory arbitration clause, ensure that the arbitration rules and forum are fair and convenient for both parties. In some cases, you may be able to negotiate for more favorable dispute resolution terms, such as a choice of venue or the right to pursue certain claims in court.

7. Non-Compliance with Legal and Regulatory Requirements

Operating a franchise requires compliance with various local, state, and federal laws and regulations. These may include labor laws, health and safety regulations, environmental requirements, and industry-specific regulations.

Pitfall: Franchisees who fail to comply with these legal and regulatory requirements can face significant penalties, including fines, legal action, or the revocation of their franchise license. Non-compliance can also damage the franchisor's brand and lead to disputes between the franchisee and franchisor.

How to Avoid It: Before opening your franchise, familiarize yourself with the legal and regulatory requirements that apply to your business. Ensure that the franchise agreement clearly outlines any legal obligations that the franchisor expects you to fulfill, and verify that the franchisor provides adequate training and support to help you meet these obligations. Additionally, consult with a legal advisor who specializes in franchise law to ensure that you remain compliant with all relevant regulations throughout the life of your franchise.

8. Not Planning for the End of the Franchise Relationship

Franchise agreements are typically long-term contracts that can last for 10 years or more. However, it's important to plan for the eventual end of the franchise relationship, whether it's through the expiration of the agreement, termination, or the sale of the business.

Pitfall: Some franchisees fail to adequately plan for what happens at the end of the franchise agreement. This can result in the loss of the business, significant financial penalties, or legal disputes over ownership of assets and intellectual property.

How to Avoid It: Review the renewal, termination, and transfer provisions in the franchise agreement carefully. Ensure that you understand what happens at the end of the franchise relationship and plan accordingly. Consider the following key aspects:

• **Renewal Provisions:** Franchise agreements typically include provisions for renewal, which may require you to meet certain performance criteria, pay renewal fees, or sign a new agreement with updated terms. It's essential to understand the renewal process well in advance of the agreement's expiration and be prepared for any changes in terms that the franchisor may impose.

• **Termination Provisions:** Understand the conditions under which the franchisor can terminate the agreement before the end of its term. Common reasons for termination include failure to meet performance standards, non-payment of royalties or fees, or violation of operational guidelines. Ensure that you have a clear understanding of your rights and obligations in the event of a termination. You may want to negotiate for a longer notice period or the opportunity to cure any default before termination occurs.

• **Post-Termination Obligations:** Many franchise agreements include post-termination obligations, such as returning proprietary materials, ceasing use of the franchisor's trademarks, and non-compete clauses that may restrict your ability to operate a similar business in the same industry. Make sure you understand these obligations and plan for how they may impact your future business endeavors.

• **Transfer and Sale of the Business:** If you decide to sell your franchise, the agreement will likely include provisions governing the transfer of ownership. These provisions may require the franchisor's approval of the buyer and the payment of transfer fees. It's important to ensure that the process for selling your business is clearly outlined and that you have the flexibility to exit the franchise system if needed. If you're considering transferring the business to family members or other successors, make sure the agreement accommodates this option.

9. Failing to Seek Professional Legal and Financial Advice

Perhaps one of the most significant legal pitfalls in franchising is failing to seek professional advice from experts who specialize in franchise law and business operations. The complexities of a franchise agreement can be overwhelming, and franchisees who do not fully understand the legal and financial implications of the agreement may find themselves facing serious consequences down the line.

Pitfall: Many franchisees attempt to navigate the legal intricacies of the franchise agreement on their own, either to save money or because they underestimate the complexity of the contract. This can lead to misinterpretations, missed opportunities for negotiation, or the failure to address key legal risks.

How to Avoid It: Engage an experienced franchise attorney to review the FDD and franchise agreement before signing. A franchise attorney can help you identify potential legal risks, negotiate more favorable terms, and ensure that your rights are protected throughout the process. Additionally, consult with a financial advisor or accountant who has experience in franchising to help you assess the financial obligations and viability of the franchise investment. By seeking professional guidance, you can avoid costly mistakes and make informed decisions that set your franchise business up for long-term success.

10. Ignoring the Importance of Ongoing Legal and Operational Compliance

The legal and operational obligations of franchisees do not end once the franchise agreement is signed. Throughout the life of the franchise, franchisees are required to comply with a range of contractual, legal, and regulatory obligations. Failure to stay compliant can lead to legal disputes, financial penalties, and even the loss of the franchise.

Pitfall: Some franchisees mistakenly believe that their legal obligations are limited to the initial phase of the franchise relationship, such as signing the agreement and paying the initial fees. However, franchising is an ongoing partnership that requires continuous compliance with the terms of the franchise agreement and external laws.

How to Avoid It: Stay proactive in maintaining compliance with both the franchise agreement and any applicable local, state, or federal regulations. This includes adhering to operational standards, making timely royalty payments, contributing to marketing funds, and meeting any performance benchmarks outlined in the agreement. Regularly review the terms of your franchise agreement and stay informed about changes in laws that may impact your business. Establish open lines of communication with the franchisor and consult with your legal or financial advisors when needed to ensure that you remain in good standing.

CONCLUSION

Navigating the legal landscape of franchising can be challenging, but with the right preparation and guidance, you can avoid the most common legal pitfalls and protect your investment. The franchise agreement is a complex, legally binding document that governs every aspect of your relationship with the franchisor. Understanding its provisions and negotiating favorable terms before signing is critical to the long-term success of your business.

By thoroughly reviewing the Franchise Disclosure Document, seeking professional legal and financial advice, and ensuring ongoing compliance with the agreement, franchisees can mitigate potential risks and avoid costly legal disputes. Key areas of concern include understanding financial obligations, protecting territorial rights, clarifying termination and renewal provisions, and planning for the end of the franchise relationship.

Ultimately, entering into a franchise agreement with a clear understanding of its legal and financial implications is one of the most important steps you can take to ensure the success of your franchise business. By being proactive and informed, you can navigate the legal pitfalls of franchising with confidence and build a strong, thriving franchise that meets your business goals.

7

NAVIGATING EARNINGS CLAIMS IN FRANCHISE AGREEMENTS

Franchise agreements are intricate legal documents that set the stage for the business relationship between the franchisor and franchisee. One of the most critical—and potentially misleading—components of a franchise agreement is the **earnings claim**. For prospective franchisees, this information can help decide whether to invest in the franchise opportunity. For franchisors, earnings claims offer a way to showcase the potential of the business. However, both sides must understand the legal requirements and implications that accompany these statements.

What Is an Earnings Claim?

An earnings claim, also known as a Financial Performance Representation (FPR), is a statement provided by the franchisor that offers insights into the potential financial performance of the franchise. It can take various forms, such as gross revenue, net profit, or even specific costs associated with operating the franchise. The purpose of an earnings claim is to give prospective franchisees an idea of what they might expect in terms of financial returns.

Franchisors are **not required** to make an earnings claim, but if they do, they must adhere to strict legal standards set forth by the Federal Trade Commission (FTC) and state laws. The key is full transparency, accuracy, and the inclusion of relevant disclaimers.

Legal Requirements for Earnings Claims

Under the FTC's **Franchise Rule**, franchisors must include any earnings claims in **Item 19** of the Franchise Disclosure Document (FDD). This requirement exists to ensure that any financial performance data shared with prospective franchisees is accurate, documented, and legally compliant. Failure to disclose earnings claims properly can lead to significant legal consequences for the franchisor, including lawsuits or fines.

Here are some of the most important legal requirements franchisors must meet:

1 DISCLOSURE IN ITEM 19: ALL EARNINGS CLAIMS MUST APPEAR IN ITEM 19 of the FDD. If the claim is mentioned elsewhere (such as in marketing materials or conversations), it must also be clearly disclosed in the FDD. The earnings claim must include the basis for the claim, such as historical data from franchisees or corporate-owned units.

2 SUBSTANTIATION: FRANCHISORS MUST PROVIDE THE DATA THAT supports their earnings claim. For example, if a franchisor claims that franchisees can make $500,000 in gross sales, they must have data to back up that assertion. This could include audited financial statements, performance data from existing franchisees, or other concrete evidence.

3 DISCLAIMERS: EARNINGS CLAIMS MUST BE ACCOMPANIED BY disclaimers, clarifying that individual results may vary. Franchisors must make it clear that the performance of each franchisee depends on a range of factors, including location, market condi-

tions, and the franchisee's operational abilities. The disclaimers should also note that past performance does not guarantee future results.

4 No Claims Without Disclosure: If a franchisor does not provide an earnings claim in Item 19 of the FDD, they cannot make any financial performance representations to prospective franchisees in conversations, emails, or marketing materials. Even a seemingly casual remark from a franchise sales representative about potential earnings can violate this rule.

5 State-Specific Requirements: In addition to FTC regulations, some states impose their own rules on earnings claims. Certain states may require additional disclosures or impose stricter regulations to protect franchisees. It's essential for franchisors to be aware of these state-specific nuances and ensure compliance.

What Franchisees Should Consider When Reviewing Earnings Claims

For prospective franchisees, earnings claims are often a key factor in the decision-making process. However, not all claims are created equal, and it's essential to approach them with a critical eye.

Here's what franchisees should consider:

1 Examine the Basis of the Claim: Earnings claims should be based on concrete, verifiable data. Franchisees should request to see the data that underpins the claim. Is the earnings information derived from corporate-owned stores, franchised locations, or both? Does the data reflect performance in markets similar to the one you are considering? The more relevant the data, the more reliable the earnings claim is likely to be.

. . .

2 Understand the Variables: Every franchise location operates under unique circumstances. Factors such as location, market competition, and the franchisee's business acumen all play a role in financial success. Franchisees should be cautious about relying solely on the earnings claim and should consider how these variables could affect their performance.

3 Ask About Averages vs. Outliers: Some earnings claims are based on averages, while others may highlight the performance of top performers. It's essential to understand whether the earnings claim represents an average or if it skews toward high-performing franchises. This distinction can help you gauge whether the earnings claim is realistic for your situation or if it's an optimistic projection.

4 Look for Hidden Costs: Earnings claims often focus on gross revenue or profit, but franchisees need to factor in the associated costs of running the business. These can include rent, wages, inventory, marketing fees, and royalties. Make sure the earnings claim provides a holistic view of the financial performance, including these expenses.

5 Consult Existing Franchisees: One of the most effective ways to evaluate the reliability of an earnings claim is by speaking with current franchisees. Ask them about their experiences, the accuracy of the earnings claim, and any unforeseen challenges they encountered. This can provide invaluable insight into whether the claim aligns with real-world performance.

. . .

6 CONSIDER THE FRANCHISOR'S SUPPORT: A STRONG SUPPORT SYSTEM can significantly impact the success of a franchise. Franchisees should assess how the franchisor's training, marketing, and ongoing support contribute to achieving the earnings potential outlined in the claim. A franchisor that offers comprehensive support increases the likelihood of reaching or exceeding the earnings claim.

7 DON'T SKIP THE FINE PRINT: PAY CLOSE ATTENTION TO THE disclaimers and footnotes that accompany the earnings claim. These often contain essential information that can alter the interpretation of the data. For example, an earnings claim might be based on a small sample size, or it might exclude franchisees who recently opened their locations.

THE RISKS OF RELYING TOO HEAVILY ON EARNINGS CLAIMS

While earnings claims can provide valuable insight into the financial potential of a franchise, they also come with risks. Franchisees who base their investment decisions solely on these claims may find themselves disappointed if their location does not perform as expected. It's crucial to view the earnings claim as one piece of a larger puzzle that includes a thorough evaluation of the franchisor, the market, and one's own abilities as a business owner.

Moreover, some franchisors may present overly optimistic or misleading earnings claims, hoping to entice prospective franchisees. This practice, while illegal, is not unheard of. Franchisees should always consult legal and financial advisors before relying on any earnings claim and ensure that they fully understand the risks involved.

CONCLUSION

Earnings claims are a powerful tool in the franchising world. For franchisors, they offer a way to demonstrate the success of their business model. For franchisees, they provide a glimpse into the potential financial rewards of owning a franchise. However, both parties must approach earnings claims with caution and ensure compliance with legal standards.

Franchisors must adhere to the FTC's disclosure requirements and substantiate their claims with solid data. Franchisees, on the other hand, should critically evaluate these claims, considering the variables that could impact their financial performance. By taking a measured, informed approach to earnings claims, both franchisors and franchisees can enter into the franchise relationship with realistic expectations and a greater chance of success.

8

PATCHWORK OF STATE FRANCHISE LAWS: UNDERSTANDING THE IMPACT ON FRANCHISE AGREEMENTS GOVERNED BY THE FTC

Franchising is often viewed as a business model governed by a uniform set of rules, particularly due to the pervasive influence of the Federal Trade Commission's (FTC) Franchise Rule. However, while the FTC Franchise Rule (16 CFR Part 436) establishes baseline requirements for the disclosure of information to prospective franchisees, franchisors and franchisees operating across the United States must navigate a complex patchwork of state-specific laws that can significantly affect franchise agreements. This chapter delves into the ways in which state laws on franchising interact with the FTC rule, influencing everything from franchise registration and disclosure requirements to the terms of franchise agreements, termination rights, and dispute resolution procedures.

I. THE ROLE OF THE FTC FRANCHISE RULE: A BASELINE FOR Uniformity

The FTC Franchise Rule, adopted in 1979 and updated in 2007, serves as the foundation of franchise law in the U.S. It mandates that franchisors provide prospective franchisees with a Franchise Disclosure Document (FDD) at least 14 days before signing a franchise agreement or receiving payment. The goal of the rule is to ensure that franchisees have sufficient information to make informed investment decisions. This federal regulation outlines 23 items that must be disclosed, including details about the franchisor's business, fees, litigation history, and financial performance representations (if provided).

Although the FTC Franchise Rule sets forth these critical protections, it does not regulate every aspect of the franchise relationship. For example, the Rule does not require franchisors to register their franchise offerings with any federal body, nor does it establish specific legal remedies or penalties for violations of the disclosure obligations. Instead, it relies on state-level enforcement and private litigation under broader deceptive trade practices laws. Consequently, state legislatures have stepped in to create their own franchise laws, some of which impose additional requirements on franchisors.

2. State Franchise Laws: Expanding on the FTC's Framework

Approximately 15 states have enacted specific franchise laws that either supplement or go beyond the FTC Franchise Rule. These states, known as "registration states" or "franchise relationship states," have developed their own systems of franchise regulation. Broadly speaking, these laws fall into two categories: **disclosure and registration laws** and **relationship laws.**

A. Disclosure and Registration States

Several states, including California, New York, Illinois, and Washington, require franchisors to register their franchise offerings with a state regulatory agency before selling franchises in that state. These states impose stricter scrutiny on franchise offers, sometimes requiring that the FDD be submitted for review and approval by a state regulatory body. Franchisors must ensure that their FDDs comply not only with federal disclosure requirements but also with additional state-specific rules.

. . .

I. CALIFORNIA

The California Franchise Investment Law (CFIL) is one of the most comprehensive state franchise statutes. Under the CFIL, franchisors must file their FDD with the California Department of Financial Protection and Innovation (DFPI) for approval before offering franchises in the state. California has historically imposed stricter requirements on FDDs, often reviewing and commenting on the content to ensure it meets the state's consumer protection standards.

For example, the CFIL mandates that financial performance representations be substantiated and clearly presented, ensuring that prospective franchisees understand the risks involved. Franchisors must also provide a detailed breakdown of the estimated initial investment costs, avoiding vague language that might mislead franchisees. Additionally, California law prohibits any earnings claims unless the franchisor has a reasonable basis for making such statements, and they must be backed by concrete data.

II. NEW YORK

New York's Franchise Sales Act similarly requires franchisors to register their franchise offers with the New York State Department of Law. The registration process includes submitting the FDD, franchise agreements, and other required documents. The state reviews the materials to ensure that they comply with New York's franchise laws, which may include provisions on earnings claims and limitations on franchise termination.

One of the most significant impacts of these registration laws is the added compliance burden for franchisors. Not only must they comply with the FTC rule, but they must also tailor their FDD and franchise agreements to satisfy the specific requirements of each state in which they plan to operate. This can result in significant legal and administrative costs for franchisors, particularly those seeking to expand nationally.

. . .

B. Franchise Relationship States

In addition to regulating franchise disclosures, many states have passed **franchise relationship laws** that govern the ongoing relationship between franchisors and franchisees. These laws address critical aspects of the franchise agreement, including termination, nonrenewal, and transfer of the franchise. Notably, these laws often impose restrictions on franchisors that go beyond the protections offered by the FTC Franchise Rule.

i. Illinois

The Illinois Franchise Disclosure Act (IFDA) not only requires the registration of franchise offerings but also imposes significant restrictions on the termination or nonrenewal of franchise agreements. Under the IFDA, a franchisor cannot terminate a franchisee without "good cause," which typically means that the franchisee has failed to comply with the terms of the franchise agreement. Moreover, the franchisor must provide the franchisee with written notice of the breach and an opportunity to cure the defect before termination. These protections are designed to prevent arbitrary or unfair termination of franchise relationships, providing franchisees with greater security in their investments.

ii. New Jersey

New Jersey's Franchise Practices Act (FPA) similarly protects franchisees from unfair termination. The FPA prohibits franchisors from terminating or failing to renew a franchise agreement without providing at least 60 days' notice and a chance for the franchisee to rectify any default. In addition, the FPA restricts the franchisor's ability to impose unreasonable transfer requirements on franchisees who wish to sell or transfer their businesses. These relationship laws provide franchisees with greater bargaining power and stability, but they also limit the flexibility of franchisors in managing their franchise networks.

. . .

3. The Interaction Between State Laws and the FTC Rule: Compliance Challenges

Franchisors seeking to operate in multiple states must carefully navigate the interplay between federal and state laws. While the FTC Franchise Rule provides a uniform set of disclosure requirements, state laws often add layers of complexity that franchisors must address. Some of the most common challenges include:

A. Variability in Registration Requirements

As previously discussed, many states require franchisors to register their FDDs before offering franchises. However, the specific requirements for registration can vary significantly from state to state. In some cases, states require extensive financial disclosures or place restrictions on certain terms in the franchise agreement. For example, some states may require that the franchise agreement include a provision allowing franchisees to litigate disputes in the state, regardless of where the franchisor is located.

In states like California and New York, franchisors may face delays in obtaining approval for their franchise registrations, as state regulators review the FDD for compliance with state laws. This can slow the expansion of a franchise network, as franchisors must wait for state approval before they can begin selling franchises.

B. State-Specific Amendments to Franchise Agreements

In addition to modifying their FDDs, franchisors may need to make state-specific amendments to their franchise agreements to comply with local laws. For instance, some states, like Virginia and Illinois, prohibit certain restrictive clauses in franchise agreements, such as clauses that limit the franchisee's right to litigate in state courts or impose excessively high transfer fees. Franchisors must ensure that their agreements are tailored to each state's requirements to avoid legal challenges from franchisees.

C. Enhanced Franchisee Protections

State franchise laws often provide franchisees with protections that go beyond the FTC Rule. For instance, in states like Washington and Maryland, franchisors may be restricted from unilaterally changing certain terms of the franchise agreement, such as fees or marketing obligations, without the franchisee's consent. These enhanced protections may require franchisors to adopt a more collaborative approach to managing their franchise networks, working closely with franchisees to ensure compliance with state laws.

4. The Importance of State-Level Compliance: Legal and Financial Risks

The legal and financial risks of non-compliance with state franchise laws can be significant. Failure to register a franchise offering in a registration state, for example, can result in penalties, fines, and even the rescission of franchise agreements. Franchisors may also face civil lawsuits from franchisees, who can claim damages if the franchisor violated state disclosure or relationship laws.

Franchisors operating in multiple states must also be mindful of the potential for conflicting laws. For example, while the FTC Franchise Rule allows franchisors to impose venue selection clauses in franchise agreements (i.e., requiring disputes to be resolved in the franchisor's home state), some state laws, such as those in California, prohibit such clauses. In these cases, franchisors must be prepared to adjust their agreements to comply with the more restrictive state law.

5. Conclusion: Striking a Balance Between Federal and State Law

In conclusion, while the FTC Franchise Rule provides the foundation for franchise regulation in the United States, franchisors must also navigate a complex web of state laws that impose additional requirements and protections. From registration and disclosure requirements to relationship laws governing termination and renewal, state laws can significantly impact the structure and terms of franchise agreements. For franchisors, understanding and complying with both federal and state regulations is essential to avoiding legal pitfalls and maintaining a successful franchise network.

Franchisees, too, must be aware of their rights under both federal and state law. The enhanced protections offered by many state franchise laws can provide franchisees with greater security in their business investments, helping to balance the power dynamic between franchisors and franchisees. Ultimately, the key to success in franchising lies in understanding and adhering to the legal framework that governs this complex business model, whether at the federal or state level.

PART III

OPERATING WITHIN THE FRANCHISE SYSTEM

9

─────────

YOUR FRANCHISE TERRITORY: WHAT YOU NEED TO KNOW

Operating within a franchise system involves adhering to specific guidelines and rules set forth by the franchisor, with one of the most critical aspects being the management and operation of your **franchise territory**. Understanding your franchise territory—its boundaries, the rights associated with it, and how to operate successfully within it—is key to the long-term success of your franchise.

In this chapter, we will explore everything you need to know about your franchise territory, including how territories are defined, the types of territories that exist, the importance of exclusivity, and strategies for maximizing profitability within your designated area. Whether you're a first-time franchisee or a seasoned business owner, having a thorough understanding of your franchise territory is essential to operating effectively within the franchise system.

I. DEFINING YOUR FRANCHISE TERRITORY

The franchise territory is the geographic area in which you, as a franchisee, are authorized to operate your business. It can be defined in several ways, depending on the franchisor's business model, the market size, and the nature of the products or services being offered. Having a clear understanding of how your territory is defined is crucial because it determines where you can operate and the extent of your competition—both from other franchisees and potentially from the franchisor itself.

There are various methods by which franchisors define territories. Some of the most common include:

• **Geographic Boundaries:** Territories can be defined by geographic markers such as city limits, counties, or states. This is common in larger franchises that operate in a variety of locations.

• **Population-Based Boundaries:** In some cases, franchise territories are defined based on population. For example, a territory might cover a certain number of people (e.g., a territory of 100,000 residents). This approach ensures that each franchisee has access to a population base that can sustain the business.

• **Radius:** Another common way to define a franchise territory is by establishing a radius around the franchisee's location. For example, a franchisee might be granted the right to operate within a 10-mile radius of their location. This method is often used when the franchise relies on foot traffic or serves a local customer base.

• **Zip Codes:** Some franchisors define territories by zip codes, with each franchisee being granted the right to operate within one or more zip codes.

Regardless of how your territory is defined, it is essential to ensure that the boundaries are clearly spelled out in the franchise agreement. Vague or poorly defined territories can lead to disputes with other franchisees or the franchisor, particularly if the territory overlaps with another location or is subject to changes later.

2. Exclusive vs. Non-Exclusive Territories

One of the most important aspects of a franchise territory is whether it is **exclusive** or **non-exclusive**. This distinction can significantly impact your business, as it determines whether or not you will face direct competition from other franchisees or company-owned locations within your territory.

A. Exclusive Territories

An **exclusive territory** means that you are the only franchisee (or franchise location) permitted to operate within that defined area. The franchisor agrees not to open any other franchise or company-owned stores within your territory, and other franchisees are prohibited from entering that area to compete directly with you.

Exclusive territories offer several key advantages:

• **Protection from Competition:** The primary benefit of an exclusive territory is that it limits competition within your market, allowing you to focus on building customer loyalty and maximizing your market share. You don't have to worry about other franchisees (or the franchisor) opening a competing location nearby.

• **Market Control:** An exclusive territory gives you greater control over the local market. This can be particularly valuable in industries where customers tend to be loyal to local businesses or where market saturation can diminish profitability.

• **Higher Potential for Growth:** With less competition, franchisees in exclusive territories may find it easier to grow their business and increase their revenue, as they are the only provider of the franchisor's products or services in the area.

However, exclusive territories can also come with some limitations. For example, the size of your territory might be restricted, and the franchisor may impose performance benchmarks that you must meet to retain exclusivity. If you fail to meet these benchmarks, the franchisor might reserve the right to reduce the size of your territory or revoke exclusivity altogether.

B. Non-Exclusive Territories

In a **non-exclusive territory**, the franchisor reserves the right to open other franchise locations or company-owned stores within the same area. This means that you could potentially face direct competition from other franchisees or from the franchisor itself.

Non-exclusive territories are more common in certain franchise models, particularly those where multiple locations can coexist without saturating the market. For example, in urban areas with high population density, it may be feasible for multiple franchises to operate within a relatively small geographic area without significantly impacting each other's business.

While non-exclusive territories offer less protection from competition, they do come with some benefits:

• **More Flexibility for Growth:** Non-exclusive territories can sometimes offer more opportunities for expansion, as the franchisor may be willing to allow you to open additional units within the area if the market can support it.

• **Lower Initial Investment:** In some cases, non-exclusive territories come with a lower initial franchise fee, as the franchisee is not guaranteed exclusivity.

If you are granted a non-exclusive territory, it's important to negotiate for additional protections where possible, such as the right of first refusal for nearby areas or restrictions on how close another location can be to yours. This can help minimize the impact of direct competition and give you the opportunity to expand if the market allows.

3. Understanding the Impact of Territorial Rights on Your Business

The rights associated with your franchise territory can have a profound effect on your ability to succeed within the franchise system. Understanding these rights—and any restrictions—is critical to maximizing your profitability and avoiding conflicts with other franchisees or the franchisor.

A. Competition from Other Franchisees

Even within exclusive territories, you may still face competition from neighboring franchisees, especially if your territory borders another franchise location. It's important to be aware of how close other franchisees are and whether their marketing efforts overlap with your territory. In some cases, franchisees may inadvertently market to customers outside their designated territory, leading to conflicts and disputes over customer bases.

To avoid issues with neighboring franchisees, it's essential to maintain open lines of communication and clearly define the boundaries of your marketing efforts. If territorial disputes arise, the franchise agreement should outline the process for resolving them, but it's often best to resolve issues amicably with your fellow franchisees before they escalate.

B. Competition from Company-Owned Stores

In some franchise systems, the franchisor retains the right to open company-owned stores, even within franchise territories. This can be a significant concern for franchisees, as company-owned stores often benefit from greater resources and direct oversight from the franchisor.

If your franchise territory is non-exclusive or if the franchisor retains the right to open company-owned locations, you should carefully review the franchise agreement to understand the extent of this right. In some cases, you may be able to negotiate for additional protections, such as a guaranteed distance between your location and any company-owned stores.

C. E-Commerce and Online Competition

As more businesses shift to online platforms, franchisees must also consider the impact of e-commerce on their territory rights. In some franchise systems, the franchisor may operate an online store that serves customers nationwide, including within your territory. This can create competition for franchisees, particularly if customers within your territory are directed to purchase products or services online rather than from your physical location.

To mitigate the impact of e-commerce competition, franchisees should clarify how online sales are handled within their territory.

Some franchisors offer franchisees a share of the revenue from online sales made within their territory, while others may allow franchisees to operate their own online store or fulfill local online orders. Negotiating these terms upfront can help ensure that you are not losing out on potential business to the franchisor's e-commerce platform.

4. Maximizing Success Within Your Franchise Territory

Operating within your designated franchise territory presents both opportunities and challenges. To maximize your success, it's important to develop a comprehensive strategy for building your customer base, managing competition, and expanding your business. Here are some key strategies for thriving within your territory:

A. Local Marketing and Community Engagement

One of the primary advantages of operating a franchise is the ability to leverage the brand recognition and marketing support provided by the franchisor. However, local marketing efforts are often the key to success in any territory. By engaging with the local community and building relationships with customers, you can create a loyal customer base that will support your business for years to come.

Consider sponsoring local events, partnering with other businesses in your community, and using targeted advertising to reach customers within your territory. The more visible and involved you are in the local community, the more likely customers are to choose your business over competitors.

B. Meeting Performance Benchmarks

Many franchisors include performance benchmarks in the franchise agreement that franchisees must meet to retain their territory or gain additional rights, such as expanding their business or opening new locations. These benchmarks often include sales targets, customer satisfaction scores, and operational standards.

To ensure that you meet (or exceed) these benchmarks, focus on delivering high-quality products and services, managing your operations efficiently, and continually improving the customer experience. Regularly review your performance metrics and seek support from the franchisor if you are struggling to meet any of the required standards.

C. Expanding Your Territory

If your franchise agreement allows for territorial expansion, this can be a valuable opportunity to grow your business and increase profitability. In some cases, franchisees can negotiate for the right of first refusal to open additional locations within nearby areas or to expand their territory if certain performance benchmarks are met. Expanding your territory can provide several advantages, including increased market share, reduced competition, and the ability to capitalize on your existing operational infrastructure.

Before pursuing territorial expansion, it's essential to conduct thorough market research to ensure that the area can support additional franchise locations or a larger service area. Factors such as population growth, local competition, and consumer demand should all be carefully evaluated. Expanding too quickly or into a market that cannot sustain your business can lead to financial strain and operational difficulties.

If you believe you are ready to expand, engage in discussions with your franchisor to outline the specific terms of your expansion. Ensure that any agreements regarding additional territory or locations are clearly documented in an addendum to your franchise agreement, including any new performance requirements or financial obligations.

D. Utilizing Franchisor Support and Resources

One of the key benefits of operating within a franchise system is the access to support and resources provided by the franchisor. These resources can be invaluable in helping you succeed within your territory, whether it's through marketing assistance, training programs, operational support, or technology tools.

To make the most of these resources, maintain open and ongoing communication with the franchisor. Don't hesitate to reach out for guidance or assistance when needed, especially if you encounter challenges within your territory. Many franchisors offer regular training and updates on best practices, and participating in these programs can help you stay ahead of the competition and ensure that you're operating efficiently.

Additionally, take advantage of any marketing or promotional campaigns that the franchisor offers. Many franchise systems have national or regional marketing efforts that can drive customer traffic to your location. Be proactive in incorporating these campaigns into your local marketing strategy to maximize their effectiveness.

E. Addressing Challenges and Adapting to Market Changes

Operating within a franchise territory is not without its challenges. Market conditions can change over time, and franchisees must be prepared to adapt to shifts in consumer behavior, economic trends, and competitive pressures. Successful franchisees remain flexible and responsive to these changes, continually seeking new ways to improve their operations and better serve their customers.

One key challenge that franchisees may face is market saturation. Even in exclusive territories, the presence of neighboring franchises or other competitors can lead to market saturation, which can impact your sales and profitability. If you begin to see diminishing returns in your territory, consider reevaluating your marketing strategies or exploring new customer segments. Expanding your product or service offerings, adjusting your pricing strategies, or enhancing the customer experience can all help you differentiate your business in a competitive market.

Another potential challenge is the impact of external factors, such as changes in local regulations, economic downturns, or shifts in consumer preferences. To stay resilient in the face of these challenges, franchisees should regularly monitor market conditions and seek input from the franchisor on how to navigate these changes. In some cases, franchisees may need to adjust their operations or marketing efforts to respond to new trends or regulations.

5. Protecting Your Franchise Territory and Legal Considerations

Protecting your franchise territory from encroachment or

disputes is an ongoing responsibility. Even if you've been granted exclusive rights to a territory, issues can arise if the boundaries are not well-defined or if other franchisees encroach on your market. Additionally, competition from company-owned locations, online sales, or third-party delivery platforms can create challenges for franchisees operating in today's digital marketplace.

A. Territorial Encroachment

Territorial encroachment occurs when another franchisee or company-owned location begins to compete within your designated territory, either intentionally or unintentionally. This can happen if your territory boundaries are not clearly defined, if neighboring franchisees engage in marketing efforts that target your customers, or if the franchisor opens a new location too close to your existing operation.

To protect against encroachment, it's essential to have a clear and enforceable definition of your territory in the franchise agreement. If encroachment does occur, address the issue with the franchisor immediately, as the franchisor is responsible for ensuring that territorial rights are respected. In some cases, the franchise agreement will include specific dispute resolution processes for addressing territorial issues, such as mediation or arbitration. It's important to follow these processes to resolve disputes amicably and efficiently.

B. E-Commerce and Online Competition

As online sales and third-party delivery platforms become more prevalent, franchisees must be vigilant about how these services affect their territorial rights. Many franchisors operate e-commerce platforms that serve customers across the country, which can lead to competition with franchisees who rely on local sales.

If your franchise system includes an e-commerce platform, it's important to clarify how revenue from online sales is allocated. In some cases, franchisors may share a portion of online sales revenue with franchisees, especially for orders fulfilled within their territory. Negotiating these terms upfront can help ensure that you are compensated for any business lost to the franchisor's online platform.

Additionally, if third-party delivery services are part of the franchisor's business model, be aware of how these services operate within your territory. Ensure that customers ordering from within your territory are directed to your location, rather than a neighboring franchisee or company-owned store.

C. Legal Protections and Consulting with a Franchise Attorney

Operating within a franchise territory involves navigating both business and legal challenges. It's critical to ensure that your territorial rights are protected and that you fully understand the legal implications of your franchise agreement. Consulting with a franchise attorney can provide valuable insight into how to safeguard your interests within the franchise system.

A franchise attorney can help you review and negotiate the territorial provisions of your franchise agreement, ensuring that your rights are clearly defined and enforceable. They can also assist with any disputes that arise, whether it's over territorial boundaries, competition, or performance benchmarks. Having legal guidance on your side can help you avoid potential pitfalls and protect your investment in the long term.

CONCLUSION

Operating within your franchise territory is a complex and multifaceted process that requires a thorough understanding of your rights, responsibilities, and the competitive landscape. Whether your territory is exclusive or non-exclusive, clearly defined or more fluid, it is essential to manage and maximize your operations within the area granted to you by the franchisor.

By understanding how your territory is defined, addressing competition from other franchisees or company-owned locations, and leveraging franchisor support and local marketing efforts, you can create a successful and thriving business within your designated area. Protecting your territorial rights, adapting to market changes, and planning for growth are all critical components of operating effectively within a franchise system.

With careful planning, ongoing communication with the franchisor, and a proactive approach to managing your business, you can maximize your profitability and achieve long-term success within your franchise territory. Ultimately, the key to success lies in understanding the unique dynamics of your territory and using that knowledge to make informed decisions that benefit your business and your customers.

10

MARKETING AND ADVERTISING REQUIREMENTS

Marketing and advertising are fundamental components of a successful franchise operation. As a franchisee, you benefit from the brand recognition and national marketing efforts of the franchisor, but you are also responsible for executing local marketing strategies that help your business grow within your territory. However, marketing in a franchise system comes with specific requirements and guidelines that must be followed to ensure brand consistency across all franchise locations.

In this chapter, we will explore the marketing and advertising requirements that franchisees must adhere to, the role of the franchisor in supporting your marketing efforts, and strategies for executing successful local campaigns. Understanding how to navigate the marketing requirements of your franchise system is essential to building a loyal customer base and maximizing the potential of your business.

1. The Role of Marketing in a Franchise System

One of the key advantages of joining a franchise system is the ability to leverage the franchisor's brand recognition, established reputation, and marketing strategies. When customers are familiar with a brand, they are more likely to trust and patronize your franchise location, which can significantly reduce the time and resources needed to build brand awareness from scratch.

Franchise systems typically include multiple layers of marketing, including national, regional, and local campaigns. Each of these plays a specific role in driving customers to franchise locations:

• **National Marketing:** The franchisor usually oversees national marketing efforts, which may include TV commercials, online campaigns, social media, sponsorships, and partnerships. These campaigns are designed to promote the brand as a whole and attract customers to all franchise locations. Franchisees benefit from these campaigns without having to organize or manage them, but they may be required to contribute to a national marketing fund to help cover the costs.

• **Regional Marketing:** In some cases, franchisors implement regional marketing campaigns that target specific geographic areas or demographics. Regional campaigns may be tailored to align with local preferences or market trends and can complement national efforts. Franchisees in a particular region may be asked to contribute to these campaigns or participate in cooperative advertising efforts.

• **Local Marketing:** While national and regional campaigns promote the brand, franchisees are often responsible for executing marketing strategies at the local level. Local marketing efforts include activities such as direct mail campaigns, local media advertising, community sponsorships, and events. These efforts help attract customers to your specific location and establish your franchise as an active part of the local community.

Understanding the role of marketing at each level is critical to operating within the franchise system, as you'll need to balance adherence to the franchisor's guidelines with the need to adapt your efforts to local market conditions.

2. Marketing Fees and Contributions

Most franchise systems require franchisees to contribute to a marketing fund that supports national or regional advertising campaigns. These contributions are typically outlined in the franchise agreement and are calculated as a percentage of gross sales. In addition to the national marketing fund, franchisees may also be required to invest in local marketing initiatives, either independently or as part of a cooperative with other franchisees in the area.

A. National Marketing Fund

The **national marketing fund** is a pool of money collected from all franchisees to support brand-wide marketing efforts. Contributions to the national marketing fund are usually non-negotiable and are set at a fixed percentage of gross sales, often ranging from 1% to 5%.

Pitfall: Some franchisees may underestimate the financial burden of marketing fees, particularly if they are operating in a highly competitive or low-margin market. Franchisees who are unaware of the ongoing nature of these fees may find themselves struggling to manage cash flow.

How to Avoid It: Carefully review the franchise agreement to understand how marketing fees are calculated and when they are due. Factor these fees into your financial planning from the outset, and be prepared for variations in marketing contributions based on fluctuations in your sales. Additionally, inquire about how the national marketing fund is managed and how funds are allocated. Transparency is essential to ensure that your contributions are being used effectively to promote the brand.

B. Local Marketing Requirements

While the franchisor may handle national and regional advertising, franchisees are usually responsible for **local marketing efforts** to drive customers to their specific location. Local marketing requirements are often outlined in the franchise agreement and may include a minimum spending requirement for advertising.

Local marketing spending typically ranges between 1% and 3% of gross sales, though this varies depending on the franchise system. Franchisees are expected to invest in advertising channels that are most effective for their local market, such as direct mail, local newspapers, radio, billboards, and digital marketing.

Pitfall: Some franchisees may focus solely on national marketing and assume it will be enough to attract customers to their location. However, without targeted local marketing efforts, franchisees may struggle to build a customer base in their immediate area.

How to Avoid It: Develop a comprehensive local marketing strategy that complements the franchisor's national campaigns. Focus on marketing channels that resonate with your local community and take advantage of any marketing materials or templates provided by the franchisor. Regularly review the results of your local marketing efforts and adjust your strategy as needed to optimize performance.

3. MARKETING GUIDELINES AND RESTRICTIONS

One of the core principles of franchising is maintaining **brand consistency** across all franchise locations. This means that while you may have some flexibility in your local marketing efforts, the franchisor will likely impose specific guidelines and restrictions to ensure that the brand's image, messaging, and presentation are consistent.

A. Brand Guidelines

Franchisors often provide franchisees with a **brand manual** or marketing guide that outlines the approved use of logos, colors, fonts, taglines, and other brand elements. These guidelines ensure that all advertising and marketing materials adhere to the franchisor's standards and that the brand is represented consistently across all locations.

Pitfall: Franchisees who fail to follow the franchisor's brand guidelines may create marketing materials that conflict with the established brand image. This can lead to customer confusion and weaken the overall brand.

How to Avoid It: Familiarize yourself with the franchisor's brand guidelines and ensure that all marketing materials, from signage to digital ads, comply with these standards. If you're unsure about whether a particular marketing campaign aligns with the franchisor's guidelines, seek approval from the franchisor's marketing department before proceeding.

B. Approval Process for Marketing Materials

Many franchisors require franchisees to submit marketing materials for **approval** before they can be used. This process helps ensure that all advertising aligns with the brand's messaging and does not conflict with national or regional campaigns. While the approval process can vary by franchise system, it often involves submitting local ads, flyers, or digital content to the franchisor's marketing team for review.

Pitfall: Delays in the approval process can slow down local marketing efforts, particularly if the franchisor takes time to review and provide feedback on submitted materials.

How to Avoid It: Plan your local marketing efforts well in advance to allow time for the approval process. Be proactive in submitting materials for review and follow up with the franchisor if there are delays. In some cases, the franchisor may provide pre-approved templates or materials that franchisees can customize for their local market, which can streamline the process.

4. LEVERAGING FRANCHISOR-SUPPORTED MARKETING INITIATIVES

One of the most valuable benefits of joining a franchise system is access to the franchisor's **marketing resources** and support. Franchisors often provide franchisees with tools and materials to help them execute local marketing campaigns more effectively. These resources may include templates for print ads, digital marketing assets, and social media content.

A. Marketing Templates and Materials

Many franchisors provide franchisees with ready-made **marketing templates** that can be customized for local use. These templates often include approved branding elements, messaging, and design, making it easy for franchisees to create professional-looking ads that align with the franchisor's brand standards. Examples of marketing materials that franchisors may provide include:

- Flyers and brochures
- Direct mail templates
- Social media graphics
- Email marketing templates
- Digital banners for websites or online ads

By using these templates, franchisees can save time and ensure that their local marketing efforts meet the franchisor's guidelines.

B. National Promotions and Campaigns

Franchisors often launch **national promotions** or seasonal campaigns that franchisees can participate in to drive sales. These promotions may include limited-time offers, discounts, or product launches that are promoted through national advertising channels. Franchisees can leverage these promotions to increase foot traffic and sales at their location.

Pitfall: Failing to participate in national promotions or misaligning local marketing with national campaigns can lead to missed opportunities to attract customers and drive revenue.

How to Avoid It: Stay informed about upcoming national promotions and incorporate them into your local marketing strategy. Align your local advertising efforts with the national campaign's messaging and take advantage of any promotional materials provided by the franchisor. Additionally, consider offering complementary local promotions or events to further engage customers and maximize the impact of the national campaign.

5. EXECUTING LOCAL MARKETING CAMPAIGNS

While the franchisor provides support and guidance, franchisees are responsible for executing **local marketing campaigns** to drive traffic to their specific location. Developing an effective local marketing strategy requires an understanding of your target audience, the local competitive landscape, and the most effective marketing channels for reaching customers in your area.

A. Understanding Your Local Market

Before launching any local marketing campaigns, it's important to

research your local market to identify key demographics, customer preferences, and competitive factors. Understanding your target audience will help you tailor your marketing efforts to resonate with local customers.

Consider conducting surveys, focus groups, or market research to gather insights into your customers' needs and preferences. Pay attention to local trends and seasonal variations in customer behavior, as these can influence the timing and content of your marketing campaigns.

B. Selecting the Right Marketing Channels

Once you've developed a clear understanding of your local market, the next step is to select the most effective **marketing channels** to reach your target audience. Depending on your business model and the demographics of your customers, some marketing channels may be more effective than others. Common local marketing channels include:

• **Direct Mail:** Direct mail campaigns can be highly effective for reaching local customers, especially if you're promoting a special offer, grand opening, or new product launch. By targeting specific neighborhoods or demographics within your territory, direct mail can help you generate immediate foot traffic to your location.

• **Local Print and Radio Advertising:** Traditional media such as local newspapers, magazines, and radio stations can be useful for building brand awareness and reaching a broad audience. However, it's important to assess whether these channels align with your target market. For example, print advertising may be effective in areas with an older population, while radio advertising could work well in communities where commuters are likely to listen to local stations.

• **Billboards and Outdoor Advertising:** If your franchise relies on a physical location with high visibility, outdoor advertising such as billboards, transit ads, or signage can increase awareness and drive traffic. Outdoor ads work particularly well for businesses located near highways or busy shopping districts.

• **Digital Marketing:** Digital marketing offers a range of options for reaching local customers online, from **social media advertising** to **pay-per-click (PPC)** ads. Platforms like Facebook, Instagram, and Google Ads allow you to target customers based on geographic location, interests, and behavior. Digital marketing can be highly effective for franchisees with a younger, tech-savvy audience.

• **Social Media:** Social media platforms like Facebook, Instagram, Twitter, and LinkedIn allow franchisees to engage with their local community, promote events, and build brand loyalty. Posting regularly about promotions, customer experiences, and community involvement can help foster a strong online presence. Many franchisors provide guidelines or templates for social media posts to ensure brand consistency.

• **Email Marketing:** Collecting customer emails and sending regular newsletters or promotions can be a powerful way to keep your audience engaged. Many customers appreciate exclusive offers or updates, and email marketing allows you to nurture relationships with loyal customers.

• **Community Involvement and Sponsorships:** One of the most effective ways to build a local customer base is by becoming involved in the community. Consider sponsoring local events, schools, or sports teams, or hosting charity events at your location. Being a visible and active participant in your community can enhance your reputation and attract loyal customers who want to support local businesses.

C. Measuring the Success of Your Marketing Campaigns

It's important to track the **effectiveness** of your local marketing campaigns to determine what works and what doesn't. By analyzing the results of each campaign, you can refine your strategy over time and maximize your return on investment (ROI).

Some key metrics to track include:

• **Foot Traffic:** How many customers visit your location during or after the campaign?

• **Sales:** Did the marketing campaign lead to an increase in sales? Which products or services saw the most growth?

• **Customer Engagement:** How did customers respond to your promotion or event? Are they engaging with your brand on social media or through other channels?

• **Customer Acquisition Cost:** How much did it cost to acquire new customers through the campaign, and does the revenue generated from those customers justify the investment?

Using tools like Google Analytics, social media insights, and point-of-sale data can help you assess the performance of your digital and offline marketing efforts. Regularly reviewing these metrics allows you to optimize your strategy, adjust your budget, and focus on the channels that yield the best results.

6. COMMON PITFALLS IN FRANCHISE MARKETING AND HOW TO Avoid Them

While franchise marketing offers numerous opportunities, there are also potential pitfalls that franchisees need to be aware of. By understanding these common challenges, you can avoid costly mistakes and ensure that your marketing efforts are both compliant and effective.

A. Overreliance on National Marketing

Some franchisees may rely too heavily on the franchisor's national marketing campaigns, assuming that these efforts alone will drive sufficient traffic to their location. However, national campaigns are often broad and may not address the specific needs of your local market.

How to Avoid It: Always supplement national campaigns with **targeted local marketing efforts.** Focus on building strong relationships with your community and tailoring your marketing to local preferences and trends.

B. Failure to Follow Brand Guidelines

Franchisees sometimes deviate from the franchisor's brand guidelines when creating local marketing materials, either because they want more creative control or because they don't fully understand the importance of maintaining consistency across all locations.

How to Avoid It: Always adhere to the franchisor's **brand guide-**

lines when creating marketing materials, and seek approval from the franchisor for any new campaigns. Ensuring brand consistency is key to maintaining the trust and recognition of the brand across all locations.

C. Not Allocating Enough Budget for Local Marketing

Many franchisees underestimate the importance of local marketing and fail to allocate enough budget toward it, focusing solely on operational expenses. Without sufficient investment in local marketing, it's challenging to grow your customer base and stand out from competitors.

How to Avoid It: Set aside a **dedicated budget** for local marketing efforts, and ensure that you are meeting any minimum spending requirements set by the franchisor. Continually assess the ROI of your campaigns and be willing to adjust your budget to support the most effective marketing strategies.

D. Ineffective Use of Marketing Channels

Using the wrong marketing channels or spreading your budget too thin across too many platforms can lead to ineffective campaigns. It's essential to focus on the channels that deliver the best results for your local market.

How to Avoid It: Conduct market research to identify the most effective marketing channels for your target audience. Focus on the platforms that are most likely to reach your customers and deliver measurable results. For example, if your audience skews younger, investing more in social media and digital marketing may be more effective than traditional print ads.

7. STAYING COMPETITIVE IN YOUR MARKET

As a franchisee, you operate within a competitive landscape that includes not only other franchises but also independent businesses in your area. To succeed, you must consistently evaluate your local market and adapt your marketing strategy to stay ahead of competitors.

A. Monitoring Competitors

Keep a close eye on your local competitors, both within and outside of the franchise system. Monitor their marketing efforts, promotions, and customer engagement strategies. Understanding what your competitors are doing can help you identify gaps in your own strategy and find opportunities to differentiate your business.

B. Differentiating Your Franchise

While consistency with the franchisor's brand is important, you can still find ways to **differentiate** your franchise location through exceptional customer service, unique local promotions, and community involvement. By building a strong local presence and offering a superior customer experience, you can create loyal customers who choose your franchise over competitors.

CONCLUSION

Marketing and advertising are critical to the success of any franchise, and operating within the franchise system means following specific guidelines while also tailoring your efforts to your local market. Understanding the role of marketing at the national, regional, and local levels is key to developing an effective strategy that drives traffic and increases sales.

By adhering to brand guidelines, leveraging franchisor-supported marketing initiatives, and executing targeted local campaigns, you can maximize the impact of your marketing efforts and build a strong customer base within your territory. Stay proactive in your marketing efforts, measure the effectiveness of your campaigns, and continually adapt to the needs of your local market to ensure long-term success within the franchise system.

11

**EMPLOYMENT LAWS AND LABOR
ISSUES IN FRANCHISING**

Franchising presents unique challenges when it comes to employment laws and labor issues. As a franchisee, you are an independent business owner responsible for managing your employees, but you also operate within a franchise system that often provides strict guidelines and policies for staffing, training, and workplace standards. Navigating the intersection of federal, state, and local employment laws while adhering to the franchisor's operational requirements can be complex.

This chapter will provide a comprehensive overview of employment laws and labor issues that are specific to franchising. We will explore topics such as employee classification, wage and hour laws, joint employer liability, workplace safety, and strategies for ensuring compliance with labor regulations. Understanding your responsibilities as an employer and how they intersect with the franchise system is essential to protecting your business from legal disputes and maintaining a productive workforce.

I. UNDERSTANDING YOUR ROLE AS AN EMPLOYER IN A FRANCHISE System

As a franchisee, you are considered the employer of your staff, even though you operate under the franchisor's brand and follow certain guidelines established by the franchisor. This means that you are responsible for hiring, training, paying, and managing your employees in accordance with applicable labor laws. While the franchisor may provide guidance and support on human resources matters, you are ultimately liable for any violations of employment laws within your franchise location.

A. Independent Business Owner

It's important to remember that franchisees are independent business owners. Although you may follow a franchisor's system for running the business, you have the autonomy to manage the day-to-day operations of your workforce, including decisions related to hiring, scheduling, payroll, and discipline.

However, the level of autonomy you have may vary depending on the franchise system. Some franchisors exert more control over employment practices through detailed manuals and operational procedures, while others give franchisees more flexibility. Regardless of the level of control, you, as the franchisee, are the employer of record.

B. Employer Responsibilities

As an employer, you must comply with a wide range of employment laws, which include but are not limited to:

- **Wage and hour regulations**
- **Anti-discrimination laws**
- **Health and safety regulations**
- **Workers' compensation laws**
- **Family and medical leave laws**
- **Immigration and employment eligibility verification**

Understanding these laws and how they apply to your business is critical to maintaining compliance and avoiding legal disputes with employees.

2. Wage and Hour Laws in Franchising

Wage and hour laws regulate the payment of wages, including minimum wage, overtime pay, and working hours. These laws are governed by the **Fair Labor Standards Act (FLSA)** at the federal level, but state and local governments may have additional requirements. Ensuring compliance with these regulations is one of the most important aspects of managing a workforce in a franchise business.

A. Minimum Wage and Overtime

The FLSA establishes a federal minimum wage, but many states and municipalities have set higher minimum wages. As a franchisee, you are required to pay your employees at least the minimum wage set by your state or local jurisdiction, if it exceeds the federal minimum. Additionally, non-exempt employees must be paid overtime—typically 1.5 times their regular hourly rate—for any hours worked beyond 40 in a workweek.

Pitfall: Some franchisees may inadvertently violate wage and hour laws by misclassifying employees as exempt from overtime or by failing to pay the proper wage. This can lead to costly lawsuits and penalties.

How to Avoid It: Ensure that you understand the specific wage and hour requirements for your location, and regularly audit your payroll practices to ensure compliance. Classify employees correctly as exempt or non-exempt based on their job duties and responsibilities. Keep detailed records of hours worked and wages paid, and implement clear policies regarding overtime.

B. Employee Classification: Independent Contractors vs. Employees

One area where franchisees can encounter legal issues is the **misclassification** of workers as independent contractors rather than employees. While independent contractors are not entitled to the same protections and benefits as employees, misclassifying workers can result in significant legal and financial consequences.

Franchisees sometimes rely on independent contractors to reduce payroll costs and avoid obligations such as overtime pay and workers' compensation insurance. However, federal and state agencies have increasingly scrutinized the use of independent contractors, and businesses that misclassify employees can face penalties.

How to Avoid It: Ensure that workers classified as independent contractors meet the legal requirements for that status. Generally, independent contractors must have more control over how they perform their work and must not be treated as employees in terms of scheduling, supervision, or work expectations. Consult with a labor attorney if you are unsure about worker classification in your franchise.

3. Joint Employer Liability

In recent years, the issue of **joint employer liability** has become a significant concern in franchising. Joint employer status arises when both the franchisor and franchisee are considered legally responsible for labor violations committed against franchise employees. This issue has led to significant legal debate, as franchisors seek to avoid being held liable for the actions of franchisees, while franchisees want to maintain control over their workforce.

A. What is Joint Employer Liability?

Joint employer liability means that both the franchisee and the franchisor can be held responsible for employment law violations. The determination of joint employer status depends on the level of control the franchisor exercises over the franchisee's employment practices. If the franchisor exerts significant control over hiring, firing, supervision, or wages, they may be considered a joint employer alongside the franchisee.

B. Recent Legal Developments

The definition of joint employer liability has been the subject of evolving legal standards in the United States. The National Labor Relations Board (NLRB) and federal courts have shifted between more expansive and narrow definitions of joint employer status over the years. Franchisees should stay informed about changes in the law that could impact their relationship with their franchisor.

How to Avoid It: To reduce the risk of joint employer liability, franchisees should maintain clear boundaries between their role as an independent employer and the franchisor's operational guidance. While it's important to follow the franchisor's system for running the business, franchisees should retain control over key employment decisions, such as hiring, setting wages, and scheduling.

4. ANTI-DISCRIMINATION LAWS AND EQUAL EMPLOYMENT Opportunity (EEO)

Franchisees must comply with federal, state, and local **anti-discrimination laws**, which protect employees from discrimination based on race, color, religion, sex, national origin, age, disability, and other protected characteristics. These laws are enforced by the **Equal Employment Opportunity Commission (EEOC)** at the federal level, but many states have additional protections that may apply.

A. Title VII of the Civil Rights Act

Title VII of the Civil Rights Act prohibits employment discrimination on the basis of race, color, religion, sex, or national origin. This law applies to employers with 15 or more employees, and franchisees must ensure that they do not engage in discriminatory practices in hiring, promotions, termination, or compensation.

B. Americans with Disabilities Act (ADA)

The **Americans with Disabilities Act (ADA)** requires employers to provide reasonable accommodations for employees with disabilities, as long as doing so does not cause undue hardship to the business. Franchisees must ensure that their workplace is accessible and that employees with disabilities have the tools and accommodations they need to perform their jobs effectively.

Pitfall: Franchisees who fail to comply with anti-discrimination laws can face lawsuits, fines, and reputational damage. Discriminatory practices, whether intentional or unintentional, can lead to costly legal battles.

How to Avoid It: Implement clear policies that promote equal employment opportunities and prohibit discrimination. Train managers and employees on the importance of diversity and inclusion in the workplace. Regularly review your hiring, promotion, and termination practices to ensure compliance with anti-discrimination laws.

5. WORKPLACE SAFETY AND HEALTH REGULATIONS

Workplace safety is another critical issue that franchisees must address. The **Occupational Safety and Health Administration (OSHA)** sets standards for workplace safety, and employers must comply with these regulations to protect their employees from hazards.

A. OSHA Requirements

OSHA requires employers to provide a safe and healthy work environment. This includes implementing safety protocols, conducting regular training, and ensuring that employees have access to protective equipment. Franchisees must also maintain records of workplace injuries and illnesses and report serious incidents to OSHA.

Pitfall: Failing to provide a safe work environment can result in fines, penalties, and workers' compensation claims. Workplace accidents can also lead to employee turnover and damage to your business's reputation.

How to Avoid It: Stay up to date with OSHA regulations and ensure that your franchise location is in compliance with all safety standards. Conduct regular safety audits, provide ongoing training to employees, and promptly address any hazards or safety concerns in the workplace.

B. Workers' Compensation

Workers' compensation laws require employers to provide insurance coverage for employees who are injured or become ill as a result of their work. This insurance covers medical expenses and lost wages for injured employees, and in return, employees are generally prohibited from suing their employer for workplace injuries.

As a franchisee, you are responsible for securing workers'

compensation insurance for your employees. Failure to comply with workers' compensation laws can lead to fines and legal liability.

How to Avoid It: Ensure that you have the appropriate workers' compensation insurance in place and that you are in compliance with state laws regarding coverage. Work with an insurance provider that specializes in small business or franchise operations to ensure adequate protection.

6. Family and Medical Leave Act (FMLA)

The **Family and Medical Leave Act (FMLA)** entitles eligible employees to take up to 12 weeks of unpaid, job-protected leave per year for certain family or medical reasons, including the birth or adoption of a child, a serious health condition, or caring for an immediate family member with a serious health condition. FMLA applies to employers with 50 or more employees, so not all franchisees may be required to comply, depending on the size of their workforce.

A. Eligibility and Coverage

Employees are eligible for FMLA leave if they have worked for the employer for at least 12 months and have logged at least 1,250 hours during the previous year. The FMLA provides job protection, meaning that employees are entitled to return to their same position (or an equivalent one) when they return from leave.

Pitfall: Failure to comply with FMLA requirements can result in lawsuits or enforcement actions by the Department of Labor. Some franchisees mistakenly deny eligible employees FMLA leave, leading to costly legal disputes.

How to Avoid It: Understand whether the FMLA applies to your franchise location based on your employee count. If it does, implement clear policies for requesting and approving FMLA leave and ensure that managers are trained to handle FMLA requests appropriately. Maintain detailed records of leave requests and approvals to avoid compliance issues.

.   .   .

7. Immigration and Employment Eligibility

As an employer, franchisees must comply with **immigration laws** by verifying the employment eligibility of all employees. The **Immigration Reform and Control Act (IRCA)** requires employers to verify the identity and work authorization of every employee hired in the United States by completing Form I-9. Employers must retain these forms for a specified period and make them available for inspection upon request.

A. Form I-9 Compliance

The I-9 form must be completed for all new employees within three days of hiring. Employers must inspect the documents presented by the employee to verify their identity and work authorization. Failure to properly complete and retain I-9 forms can result in penalties from U.S. Immigration and Customs Enforcement (ICE).

Pitfall: Some franchisees may overlook proper I-9 compliance, particularly when managing a high-volume, high-turnover workforce. Failure to complete I-9 forms correctly can lead to fines or, in more serious cases, criminal charges for knowingly employing unauthorized workers.

How to Avoid It: Establish a formal process for completing I-9 forms for every new hire. Train managers and HR personnel to review identification documents thoroughly and complete the form accurately. Periodically audit your I-9 forms to ensure compliance with federal regulations. If you have any questions about I-9 compliance, consult with an immigration attorney.

B. E-Verify

Some states require employers to use the **E-Verify** system to confirm the work eligibility of new hires. E-Verify is an online system that compares information from an employee's I-9 form with federal records to verify their eligibility to work in the U.S. Even if it's not required by your state, you may choose to use E-Verify voluntarily to ensure compliance with immigration laws.

How to Avoid It: If your state requires the use of E-Verify, integrate the system into your hiring process and ensure that your team understands how to use it. If E-Verify is voluntary in your area, consider the benefits of using it as part of your compliance efforts.

8. Preventing and Addressing Labor Disputes

Labor disputes can arise in any business, but franchisees must take extra precautions to avoid conflicts with employees that could lead to lawsuits, regulatory investigations, or damage to the franchise brand. Common sources of labor disputes include wage and hour violations, discrimination claims, wrongful termination, and safety issues.

A. Implementing Clear HR Policies

One of the best ways to prevent labor disputes is to establish and communicate clear human resources policies that outline employee rights, workplace expectations, and procedures for resolving complaints. These policies should cover key areas such as wages, working hours, overtime, harassment, discrimination, and discipline.

How to Avoid It: Provide employees with an up-to-date employee handbook that outlines all workplace policies and procedures. Make sure employees understand their rights and responsibilities, and offer training to managers on how to handle employee complaints and grievances effectively.

B. Mediation and Arbitration

Many franchise agreements include **mediation or arbitration clauses** to resolve disputes between franchisees and their employees without going to court. These alternative dispute resolution methods can be faster and less expensive than litigation, and they can help protect the reputation of the franchise system.

How to Avoid It: Review your franchise agreement and employment contracts to determine if mediation or arbitration is required in the event of a labor dispute. If these options are available, work with your legal counsel to ensure that any disputes are handled through the appropriate channels and that you are prepared to engage in mediation or arbitration if necessary.

· · ·

9. Training and Development

Training your employees effectively is a critical part of running a successful franchise. Not only does proper training help you maintain high operational standards, but it also ensures that your employees are aware of their rights and your obligations under employment laws. Many franchisors provide training programs for franchisees, covering topics such as customer service, food safety, or retail operations, but you should also implement training programs specific to labor laws and workplace compliance.

A. Onboarding and Continuous Training

From the moment you hire an employee, they should receive comprehensive onboarding training that includes an overview of workplace policies, safety procedures, and legal compliance. Ongoing training should also be provided to ensure employees stay up-to-date on changes in labor laws, safety regulations, and company policies.

How to Avoid It: Create a structured onboarding program for new hires that covers both operational training and compliance with employment laws. Offer regular training sessions for existing employees on issues such as workplace safety, anti-harassment policies, and wage and hour rules. Document all training sessions and maintain records of employee participation.

B. Manager Training

Managers play a key role in ensuring that your franchise complies with employment laws. They are often responsible for enforcing policies, handling employee complaints, and managing day-to-day operations. It is essential to train your managers thoroughly on employment law compliance, including wage and hour regulations, anti-discrimination policies, and FMLA requirements.

How to Avoid It: Invest in training programs for managers that focus on HR compliance, conflict resolution, and employee management. Ensure that managers are aware of the legal implications of their decisions and actions, particularly when it comes to hiring, firing, and discipline.

. . .

CONCLUSION

Operating within the franchise system requires franchisees to navigate a complex array of employment laws and labor issues while maintaining compliance with the franchisor's operational standards. As an employer, you are responsible for managing your workforce, ensuring compliance with wage and hour laws, preventing discrimination, and providing a safe work environment.

By understanding the legal landscape of employment laws, including joint employer liability, FMLA requirements, and OSHA regulations, you can protect your business from costly labor disputes and regulatory penalties. Implementing clear HR policies, providing comprehensive training, and staying informed about changes in labor laws will help you maintain a compliant and productive workforce.

Ultimately, your success as a franchisee depends not only on how well you run your business but also on how effectively you manage your employees and navigate the complex world of labor regulations. By staying proactive and informed, you can mitigate risks, avoid legal pitfalls, and build a positive, compliant workplace within the franchise system.

PART IV

MANAGING DISPUTES AND EXITING THE FRANCHISE RELATIONSHIP

12

DISPUTE RESOLUTION: AVOIDING AND ADDRESSING CONFLICTS

Disputes are an inevitable part of any business relationship, and franchising is no exception. The nature of the franchisor-franchisee relationship, with its defined rights and obligations under a legal contract, means that conflicts can arise from misunderstandings, unmet expectations, or breaches of the franchise agreement. These disputes can range from issues related to royalty payments and marketing obligations to more serious matters like encroachment on territory rights or termination of the franchise agreement.

When conflicts arise, it is essential to have a well-defined approach to resolving them efficiently and effectively. The goal should always be to minimize disruption to your business, preserve the franchisor-franchisee relationship when possible, and avoid costly litigation. This chapter will explore the common causes of franchise disputes, the dispute resolution mechanisms typically included in franchise agreements, and strategies for resolving conflicts before they escalate. By understanding how to navigate disputes, you can protect your business, minimize financial risk, and maintain a positive working relationship with your franchisor.

. . .

COMMON CAUSES OF FRANCHISE DISPUTES

Franchise disputes can arise for many reasons, but the most common causes often involve issues of performance, compliance with the franchise agreement, and disagreements over business operations. Below are some of the most frequent sources of conflict between franchisors and franchisees:

1. FINANCIAL DISPUTES

Financial disagreements are among the most common sources of tension between franchisors and franchisees. These disputes can arise in several areas, including:

- **Royalty Fees:** Franchisees may dispute the calculation of royalty fees, particularly if the franchisor's definition of "gross sales" is unclear or if franchisees believe they are being overcharged. Royalty disputes can also occur if a franchisee is struggling financially and falls behind on payments.

- **Marketing Fees:** Franchisees may feel that the marketing fees they contribute to the franchisor's advertising fund are not being spent effectively or that they are not receiving an adequate return on investment from the franchisor's national or regional marketing campaigns.

- **Cost of Supplies:** Franchise agreements often require franchisees to purchase goods or services from approved suppliers. Disputes can arise if franchisees believe that the cost of these supplies is unreasonably high or if they wish to source products from alternative vendors.

2. PERFORMANCE AND COMPLIANCE ISSUES

Operational disputes often stem from disagreements over how the franchisee is running their business and whether they are complying with the franchisor's standards. These issues may include:

- **Operational Standards:** Franchisees are required to adhere to the franchisor's established **standard operating procedures (SOPs)**, which dictate everything from how products are prepared to how customer service is handled. Disputes may arise if the franchisor believes the franchisee is not meeting these standards, while the franchisee may argue that the expectations are unreasonable or that the SOPs are not effective in their particular market.

- **Brand Compliance:** Franchisees are expected to maintain the brand image and follow the franchisor's guidelines for marketing, signage, uniforms, and overall brand presentation. Disputes can arise if a franchisee deviates from these guidelines or if the franchisor enforces changes that the franchisee disagrees with.

- **Sales Performance:** Some franchise agreements include performance benchmarks that franchisees must meet, such as minimum sales targets. If a franchisee consistently fails to meet these targets, the franchisor may issue warnings or seek to terminate the agreement. Disagreements can arise over the fairness of these benchmarks or the franchisee's ability to meet them in their specific market.

3. TERRITORY ENCROACHMENT

Territorial disputes are particularly common in franchise systems that grant franchisees **exclusive territories.** These disputes often occur when franchisees believe that the franchisor or other franchisees are **encroaching** on their designated territory by opening competing locations nearby or allowing other franchisees to market within their area.

- **Territory Boundaries:** If the franchise agreement does not clearly define the territory boundaries, or if the boundaries are subject to change based on market conditions, disputes can arise over whether a new location violates the existing franchisee's territory rights.

- **Encroachment by the Franchisor:** In some cases, franchisors may open company-owned locations or sell additional franchises in areas that franchisees believe should be protected. This can lead to disputes over lost revenue and market share.

. . .

4. Termination and Renewal Issues

The **termination** or **non-renewal** of a franchise agreement is one of the most contentious areas of the franchisor-franchisee relationship. Termination disputes typically occur when the franchisor believes the franchisee has breached the terms of the agreement, while the franchisee may argue that the termination is unjustified.

• **Grounds for Termination:** Franchise agreements often include specific grounds for termination, such as failure to pay royalties, failure to comply with operational standards, or failure to meet sales targets. Franchisees may dispute the validity of the termination if they believe they have corrected the issue or if they believe the franchisor has acted in bad faith.

• **Non-Renewal:** At the end of the franchise term, the franchisee may seek to renew the agreement. Disputes can arise if the franchisor refuses to renew the agreement, especially if the franchisee believes they have met all the necessary renewal criteria.

5. Misrepresentation Claims

In some cases, franchisees may feel that they were **misled** during the sales process or that the franchisor made promises that were not fulfilled. These disputes often involve claims that the franchisor made false or misleading representations about the profitability of the franchise, the level of support provided, or the overall success of the franchise system.

• **Franchise Disclosure Document (FDD) Issues:** Franchisees may claim that the franchisor failed to provide accurate or complete information in the Franchise Disclosure Document (FDD), leading them to enter the franchise agreement under false pretenses.

• **Franchise Sales Promises:** Franchisees may also allege that the franchisor's sales team made verbal promises or assurances that were not included in the final franchise agreement, leading to disputes over what the franchisee was led to believe.

. . .

Dispute Resolution Mechanisms in Franchise Agreements

Most franchise agreements include **dispute resolution provisions** that outline how conflicts between the franchisor and franchisee will be handled. These provisions are designed to prevent disputes from escalating into costly and time-consuming litigation. Common dispute resolution mechanisms include **negotiation, mediation, arbitration**, and, in some cases, **litigation**.

1. Direct Negotiation

The first step in resolving a franchise dispute is often **direct negotiation** between the franchisor and the franchisee. Many franchise agreements include a clause requiring the parties to attempt to resolve the dispute through good-faith negotiations before resorting to more formal dispute resolution mechanisms.

Advantages of Negotiation:

- **Preserves Relationships:** Direct negotiation allows both parties to address their concerns and work toward a resolution without damaging the franchisor-franchisee relationship.

- **Cost-Effective:** Negotiating a resolution is far less expensive than going through arbitration or litigation.

- **Flexible Solutions:** The parties have more flexibility to craft a solution that meets both of their needs, rather than relying on a third-party arbitrator or judge to decide the outcome.

Challenges of Negotiation:

- **Power Imbalance:** In some cases, franchisees may feel that the franchisor holds more power in the negotiation process, especially if the franchisee is reliant on the franchisor for ongoing support and resources.

- **Lack of Enforcement:** If negotiations fail, there is no legal mechanism to enforce any agreements reached during the process.

. . .

2. MEDIATION

If direct negotiation fails, the next step is often **mediation**. Mediation is a voluntary process in which a neutral third party, known as a **mediator**, facilitates discussions between the franchisor and franchisee in an attempt to help them reach a mutually acceptable resolution.

Advantages of Mediation:

• **Neutral Facilitator:** The mediator is an impartial third party who can help both sides see the other's perspective and encourage compromise.

• **Confidentiality:** Mediation is a confidential process, meaning that the details of the dispute and any settlement agreements are not made public.

• **Non-Binding:** Mediation is a non-binding process, meaning that either party can walk away from the mediation without being forced to accept the proposed resolution.

Challenges of Mediation:

• **Voluntary Nature:** Because mediation is non-binding, there is no guarantee that the parties will reach an agreement. If one party is unwilling to compromise, mediation may fail.

• **No Legal Precedent:** Since mediation does not involve a formal legal process, the outcome does not create any legal precedent that can be used in future disputes.

3. ARBITRATION

Arbitration is a more formal dispute resolution process in which a neutral third party, known as an **arbitrator**, hears both sides of the dispute and renders a binding decision. Many franchise agreements include an **arbitration clause** requiring the parties to resolve their disputes through arbitration rather than litigation.

Advantages of Arbitration:

• **Binding Decision:** The arbitrator's decision is legally binding, meaning that both parties must comply with the outcome.

• **Faster and Less Expensive:** Arbitration is generally faster and less expensive than litigation, making it an attractive option for resolving franchise disputes.

• **Private Process:** Like mediation, arbitration is a private process, meaning that the details of the dispute are not made public.

Challenges of Arbitration:

• **Limited Appeal Rights:** One of the most significant challenges of arbitration is that the decision is usually **final and binding**, with very limited grounds for appeal. Unlike in a court case, where the losing party can appeal the decision to a higher court, arbitration rulings are difficult to overturn, even if one party believes the arbitrator made an error.

• **Potential for Bias:** In some cases, franchisees may feel that the arbitration process favors the franchisor, especially if the arbitrator has prior experience working with large franchisors or if the arbitration clause designates a specific arbitration body known to favor corporate interests. While arbitrators are expected to be neutral, the perception of bias can still be an issue.

• **Costs Can Accumulate:** While arbitration is generally less expensive than litigation, it can still be costly, particularly if the arbitration process drags on or if multiple arbitration sessions are required. Franchisees may also have to bear the costs of hiring legal representation and paying arbitration fees.

4. LITIGATION

Although most franchise agreements include clauses that require disputes to be resolved through negotiation, mediation, or arbitration, there are situations where **litigation** becomes necessary. Litigation involves taking the dispute to court, where a judge or jury will hear the case and render a decision. This is often seen as a last resort due to the time, cost, and potential damage to the franchisor-franchisee relationship.

Advantages of Litigation:

• **Comprehensive Legal Process:** Litigation allows for a thorough legal examination of the dispute, including **discovery** (the process of gathering evidence) and testimony from witnesses. This can be particularly valuable in complex disputes where extensive documentation or third-party testimony is needed to resolve the conflict.

- **Right to Appeal:** Unlike arbitration, litigation offers the opportunity for **appeal**. If either party believes the court made a legal error, they can appeal the decision to a higher court.

- **Public Accountability:** Since litigation occurs in a public forum, it can bring attention to systemic issues within the franchise system. In some cases, this can pressure the franchisor to settle disputes more fairly, as they may wish to avoid negative publicity.

Challenges of Litigation:

- **Time-Consuming:** Litigation can take **years** to resolve, especially if the case goes through multiple appeals. This can create significant uncertainty for both the franchisee and the franchisor, delaying the resolution of the dispute and prolonging business disruption.

- **Expensive:** The costs of litigation can be prohibitive, particularly for franchisees. Legal fees, court costs, and other expenses can quickly accumulate, making litigation a financially risky option.

- **Damaged Relationships:** Litigation often leads to an adversarial relationship between the franchisor and franchisee, making it difficult to continue working together after the dispute is resolved. This can be especially problematic for franchisees who are still bound by the franchise agreement and need ongoing support from the franchisor.

Steps to Avoid Franchise Disputes

While disputes are sometimes unavoidable, there are steps that franchisees can take to reduce the likelihood of conflicts and maintain a positive relationship with the franchisor.

1. Understand the Franchise Agreement

One of the most effective ways to avoid disputes is to thoroughly

understand the franchise agreement before signing it. Franchise agreements are legally binding contracts that outline the rights and obligations of both the franchisor and the franchisee. By carefully reviewing the agreement, asking questions, and seeking legal advice from a franchise attorney, you can avoid misunderstandings and ensure that you fully understand your responsibilities.

• **Key Areas to Review**: Pay special attention to areas such as royalties and fees, territory rights, performance benchmarks, renewal and termination provisions, and dispute resolution mechanisms. Ensure that any verbal promises made by the franchisor are included in the written agreement.

• **Negotiate Where Possible**: While many franchise agreements are non-negotiable, there may be opportunities to negotiate certain terms, such as territory size or renewal conditions. Addressing potential areas of concern before signing the agreement can prevent disputes later on.

2. Maintain Open Communication

Effective communication is key to preventing disputes from escalating. Franchisees should establish and maintain regular lines of communication with the franchisor, including participating in **franchisee meetings**, responding to requests for feedback, and seeking clarification on any issues that arise. By fostering a cooperative relationship, franchisees can address concerns early and work with the franchisor to find solutions.

• **Document Communications**: It's a good idea to document important communications with the franchisor, particularly if the discussion involves performance issues, compliance concerns, or requests for support. Keeping a record of these communications can be helpful if a dispute arises later.

3. Follow the Franchise System

One of the main benefits of franchising is that it provides franchisees with a proven business model. However, failing to adhere to the **franchise system** can lead to conflicts with the franchisor. Franchisees should make every effort to follow the operational procedures, branding guidelines, and marketing strategies outlined by the franchisor.

• **Stay Compliant:** Regularly review the franchisor's policies and procedures to ensure that you are in compliance. If you encounter operational challenges, reach out to the franchisor for support rather than making changes to the system on your own.

• **Seek Support When Needed:** If you are struggling to meet sales targets or comply with operational standards, don't hesitate to seek help from the franchisor. Most franchisors offer ongoing support to help franchisees succeed, and addressing issues early can prevent them from becoming disputes.

4. Be Proactive About Dispute Resolution

If a dispute does arise, taking a **proactive approach** to resolving the conflict can help prevent the situation from escalating. By addressing the issue early and working with the franchisor to find a solution, franchisees can avoid more formal and adversarial dispute resolution processes like arbitration or litigation.

• **Engage in Negotiation or Mediation:** Whenever possible, try to resolve disputes through **negotiation** or **mediation** before resorting to more formal mechanisms. These processes are less costly, less time-consuming, and more likely to result in a mutually beneficial resolution.

• **Know Your Legal Rights:** While it's always best to try to resolve disputes amicably, franchisees should also be aware of their legal rights under the franchise agreement and applicable laws. If you believe the franchisor is acting in bad faith or violating the terms of the agreement, consult with a franchise attorney to determine your options.

· · ·

CONCLUSION

Disputes are an inevitable part of the franchisor-franchisee relationship, but they don't have to result in costly litigation or damage the long-term viability of the business. By understanding the common causes of disputes, being aware of the dispute resolution mechanisms available, and taking steps to address conflicts early, franchisees can protect their businesses and maintain a positive working relationship with their franchisors.

Whether the dispute involves financial disagreements, territory issues, or compliance concerns, the key is to approach the situation with a willingness to resolve the conflict in a way that benefits both parties. By being proactive, communicative, and informed, you can navigate disputes effectively and ensure the continued success of your franchise.

13

FRANCHISE TERMINATION: HOW AND WHEN IT CAN HAPPEN

The termination of a franchise agreement is one of the most contentious and disruptive events in the franchisor-franchisee relationship. Unlike the natural expiration of a franchise term, which allows both parties to plan for the future, termination often occurs due to conflict, non-compliance, or perceived failures on the part of the franchisee. The legal and financial ramifications of a terminated franchise can be devastating for a franchisee who has invested significant time, effort, and money into building their business. For franchisors, termination may be necessary to protect the brand and the integrity of the system, but it also risks alienating other franchisees and creating negative publicity.

This chapter delves into the different aspects of franchise termination: the reasons it occurs, how termination provisions are structured in franchise agreements, what legal rights franchisees have during the termination process, and how to avoid termination in the first place. Whether you are a franchisee facing possible termination or a prospective franchisee trying to understand the risks, it's crucial to know your rights and responsibilities under the franchise agreement. By understanding the termination process and how to prevent disputes from escalating to this point, you can protect your investment and your business.

WHAT IS FRANCHISE TERMINATION?

Franchise termination occurs when the franchisor ends the franchise relationship before the expiration of the franchise agreement. Termination is often triggered by a breach of contract on the part of the franchisee, such as failure to comply with the franchisor's operational standards, failure to pay royalties, or failure to meet sales performance requirements. When a franchise agreement is terminated, the franchisee is usually required to cease all operations immediately, including stopping the use of the franchisor's trademarks and intellectual property.

Franchise agreements are legally binding contracts, and termination is a serious legal action that can have significant consequences for both parties. For the franchisee, termination can mean the loss of their business, financial penalties, and potential legal disputes. For the franchisor, terminating a franchise can harm the brand's reputation, lead to costly litigation, and create distrust among other franchisees.

REASONS FOR FRANCHISE TERMINATION

The reasons for franchise termination can vary depending on the specific terms of the franchise agreement, but most agreements include provisions that outline specific grounds for termination. It's important for franchisees to understand these provisions and to ensure they are in compliance with the franchisor's expectations at all times.

Here are some of the most common reasons for franchise termination:

.   .   .

1. Failure to Comply with Operational Standards

One of the primary responsibilities of a franchisee is to operate their business in strict accordance with the **standard operating procedures (SOPs)** set by the franchisor. These procedures are designed to maintain consistency across the entire franchise system and ensure that customers have the same experience no matter which franchise location they visit.

Failure to comply with operational standards can include issues such as:

- Not following the franchisor's guidelines for product preparation, presentation, or service delivery.
- Failing to maintain the required level of cleanliness, safety, or customer service.
- Operating outside of the brand's image, such as using unapproved advertising or deviating from the franchisor's marketing guidelines.

When a franchisee consistently fails to meet these standards, the franchisor may issue **default notices** requiring the franchisee to correct the issues. If the franchisee fails to rectify the problems within the allotted **cure period**, the franchisor may have grounds to terminate the agreement.

2. Failure to Pay Royalties or Fees

Franchisees are required to pay **ongoing royalties** and other fees, such as **marketing contributions** and **technology fees**, as outlined in the franchise agreement. These payments are usually made on a monthly or quarterly basis and are often based on the franchisee's gross sales.

Failure to pay royalties or fees is one of the most straightforward grounds for termination. Franchise agreements typically include provisions that give the franchisor the right to terminate the agreement if the franchisee falls behind on payments and fails to remedy the situation within a specified time frame.

. . .

3. Violation of Territorial Rights

Territory disputes can also lead to termination if the franchisee violates the terms of their **exclusive territory** agreement. For example, if a franchisee operates or markets outside of their designated territory or competes with other franchisees by encroaching on their territory, the franchisor may have grounds for termination.

4. Breach of Confidentiality or Non-Compete Agreements

Franchisees are often required to sign **confidentiality agreements** and **non-compete clauses** as part of the franchise agreement. These clauses are designed to protect the franchisor's proprietary information, such as trade secrets, operational methods, and intellectual property. If a franchisee breaches these agreements by sharing confidential information or starting a competing business, the franchisor can terminate the agreement and seek legal remedies.

5. Poor Financial Performance

While poor financial performance alone is not always grounds for termination, some franchise agreements include **performance benchmarks** that franchisees must meet. If a franchisee consistently fails to meet minimum sales targets or revenue requirements, the franchisor may issue warnings and, ultimately, terminate the agreement if the franchisee cannot improve their performance.

6. Legal or Regulatory Violations

Franchisees are required to comply with all relevant **local, state, and federal laws** that govern their business, including employment laws, health and safety regulations, and tax obligations. If a franchisee is found to be in violation of these laws or regulations, the franchisor may have the right to terminate the agreement to protect the brand's reputation and ensure compliance across the system.

. . .

Termination Provisions in Franchise Agreements

The termination provisions in a franchise agreement outline the specific circumstances under which the franchisor can terminate the agreement, as well as the procedures that must be followed. These provisions are crucial for both parties, as they define the legal framework for ending the franchise relationship and ensure that both the franchisor and franchisee understand their rights and obligations.

Here are some key components of franchise termination provisions:

1. Grounds for Termination

Franchise agreements typically list specific **grounds for termination**, including the reasons mentioned earlier in this chapter (e.g., failure to comply with operational standards, failure to pay royalties, breach of confidentiality, etc.). These grounds are designed to protect the franchisor's interests and ensure that franchisees are operating their businesses in accordance with the brand's standards.

2. Notice and Cure Period

Most franchise agreements include a **notice and cure period** provision, which requires the franchisor to provide the franchisee with written notice of any defaults or breaches of the agreement. The franchisee is then given a specified amount of time, known as the **cure period,** to correct the issue. If the franchisee fails to remedy the problem within the cure period, the franchisor may proceed with termination.

For **example,** if a franchisee fails to pay royalties, the franchisor may send a notice of default and give the franchisee 30 days to make the payment. If the payment is not made within the 30-day cure period, the franchisor can terminate the agreement.

. . .

3. Immediate Termination

In some cases, the franchisor may have the right to terminate the agreement **immediately**, without providing a cure period. Immediate termination is typically reserved for severe breaches of the agreement, such as:

- **Criminal activity** or fraud on the part of the franchisee.
- **Insolvency** or bankruptcy.
- Significant violations of the franchisor's operational or brand standards that damage the reputation of the brand.

Immediate termination clauses are designed to protect the franchisor from franchisees who engage in conduct that could harm the entire franchise system.

4. Post-Termination Obligations

Once a franchise agreement is terminated, the franchisee is required to comply with certain **post-termination obligations**. These obligations are designed to protect the franchisor's intellectual property and ensure a smooth transition following the termination. Common post-termination obligations include:

- **Ceasing operations:** The franchisee must immediately stop operating the business and cease using the franchisor's trademarks, logos, and branding.
- **Returning proprietary materials:** The franchisee is typically required to return all proprietary materials, such as operations manuals, marketing materials, and customer lists.
- **Non-compete obligations:** The franchisee may be bound by a **non-compete clause** that prevents them from operating a similar business within a certain geographic area for a specified period of time.

Legal Recourse for Wrongful Termination

In some cases, franchisees may believe that the franchisor has wrongfully terminated the franchise agreement. **Wrongful termination** occurs when the franchisor terminates the agreement without just cause or fails to follow the termination procedures outlined in the agreement.

Franchisees who believe they have been wrongfully terminated may have legal recourse, including:

• **Breach of contract claims:** Franchisees can file a breach of contract lawsuit if they believe the franchisor has violated the terms of the franchise agreement by terminating the agreement without proper cause or notice.

• **Unfair termination laws:** Some states have **franchise relationship laws** that provide additional protections for franchisees, such as requiring "good cause" for termination or providing franchisees with additional notice or cure periods.

• **Damages and compensation:** If a franchisee successfully proves wrongful termination, they may be entitled to damages, including compensation for lost profits, the value of their investment, and attorney fees.

It's essential for franchisees to consult with a qualified **franchise attorney** if they believe they have been wrongfully terminated. An attorney can review the franchise agreement, assess the validity of the termination, and advise on the best course of action.

Avoiding Franchise Termination

While understanding the legal rights and processes surrounding franchise termination is crucial, it's equally important to take proactive steps to avoid termination in the first place. By maintaining compliance with your franchise agreement, fostering strong communication with your franchisor, and addressing issues early, you can greatly reduce the risk of termination.

1. MAINTAIN OPEN AND TRANSPARENT COMMUNICATION

One of the most effective ways to avoid franchise termination is to maintain **open communication** with your franchisor. Building a strong relationship with your franchisor allows you to address small problems before they escalate into larger disputes.

• **Seek Guidance:** If you're facing operational challenges, struggling with compliance, or unsure about a requirement in the franchise agreement, don't hesitate to reach out to your franchisor for guidance. Franchisors have a vested interest in your success and may provide additional training, resources, or support to help you get back on track.

• **Provide Feedback:** Let your franchisor know if you believe certain operational guidelines, marketing strategies, or business expectations aren't working in your particular market. While you must still adhere to the franchise system, many franchisors value constructive feedback and may be open to adjustments or accommodations.

• **Document Issues:** If you experience challenges or disputes, document all communications and actions taken. Having a clear record of your efforts to resolve problems can be invaluable if conflicts escalate and termination becomes a possibility.

2. ADHERE TO OPERATIONAL STANDARDS

Franchise systems thrive on **consistency**—the ability to provide the same products, services, and customer experiences across all locations. Adhering to your franchisor's **standard operating procedures (SOPs)** and **brand guidelines** is key to maintaining your standing within the system and avoiding termination.

• **Regularly Review SOPs:** Operational standards may evolve over time as the franchisor updates procedures or introduces new products and services. Stay up-to-date by regularly reviewing any changes to the SOPs and implementing them promptly.

• **Conduct Internal Audits:** Conduct periodic internal audits of your business operations to ensure compliance with the franchisor's standards. This proactive approach can help you identify potential issues before they become grounds for termination.

- **Seek Training:** If you or your staff are struggling to meet the franchisor's standards, request additional training or support. Many franchisors offer refresher courses, ongoing training programs, or on-site visits from field consultants to help franchisees maintain compliance.

3. Stay Current with Financial Obligations

Failing to meet your **financial obligations**—whether it's royalty payments, marketing contributions, or technology fees—is one of the quickest ways to face franchise termination. To avoid financial disputes, it's essential to maintain accurate records and stay on top of your payments.

- **Automate Payments:** If possible, set up automated payments for royalties and other recurring fees. This can help ensure that payments are made on time and reduce the risk of falling behind.

- **Monitor Cash Flow:** Keep a close eye on your business's cash flow and plan for periods when revenue may be lower (such as seasonal slowdowns). This will help you avoid missing payments or accumulating debt.

- **Communicate Financial Challenges:** If you're experiencing financial difficulties and struggling to make payments, communicate openly with your franchisor. Some franchisors may offer temporary payment deferrals or adjustments to help you get through a challenging period.

4. Resolve Territory Issues Early

Territory disputes, especially in systems with **exclusive territories**, can quickly escalate if not addressed early. If you believe the franchisor or another franchisee is encroaching on your territory, it's important to address the issue immediately.

- **Clarify Territory Boundaries:** Ensure that your franchise agreement clearly defines your territory and any protections against encroachment. If the boundaries are vague or if the franchisor retains the right to adjust territories, clarify this with your franchisor before a conflict arises.

• **Monitor Encroachment:** Keep an eye on new developments, such as the opening of new franchise locations near your territory. If you believe your territory is being infringed upon, raise the issue with the franchisor and refer to the agreement's territory protection provisions.

• **Seek Mediation:** If territory disputes arise between you and another franchisee, consider seeking mediation to resolve the issue before escalating it to the franchisor or legal action.

5. Be Proactive About Performance

Many franchise agreements include **performance benchmarks**, such as sales targets or customer satisfaction scores, that franchisees must meet. Failing to meet these benchmarks consistently can lead to warnings, default notices, and ultimately, termination.

• **Monitor Your Metrics:** Regularly review your sales, customer feedback, and other key performance indicators (KPIs) to ensure that you are meeting the franchisor's expectations. Set internal goals to meet or exceed the performance benchmarks outlined in your franchise agreement.

• **Seek Support for Underperformance:** If your business is struggling to meet sales targets, reach out to your franchisor for support. Many franchisors offer marketing assistance, training, or operational reviews to help franchisees improve their performance.

• **Plan for Market Variability:** Recognize that market conditions can change, affecting your ability to meet performance benchmarks. If external factors (such as economic downturns, competition, or shifts in consumer demand) are impacting your performance, communicate this to your franchisor and discuss potential adjustments to the benchmarks.

6. Understand the Renewal Process

Even if termination is not an immediate concern, it's important to plan for the eventual **renewal** of your franchise agreement. Franchise agreements typically have a finite term (e.g., 5, 10, or 20 years), and franchisees must meet certain conditions to renew the agreement at the end of the term. Failure to plan for renewal can result in non-renewal, which may be functionally similar to termination.

• **Review Renewal Terms:** Familiarize yourself with the renewal provisions in your franchise agreement, including any requirements you must meet to qualify for renewal (e.g., compliance with operational standards, financial obligations, and performance benchmarks).

• **Prepare in Advance:** Begin planning for renewal well in advance of the agreement's expiration. Ensure that you have met all the renewal criteria and that your business is in good standing with the franchisor.

• **Negotiate Renewal Terms:** If you wish to negotiate any changes to the terms of the renewal, such as territory size, royalty percentages, or other obligations, begin those discussions early. This will give you time to reach an agreement with the franchisor before the renewal deadline.

Conclusion: Safeguarding Your Business

Franchise termination is a serious and potentially devastating event, but it is not inevitable. By understanding the reasons for termination, adhering to the terms of your franchise agreement, and taking proactive steps to address challenges before they escalate, you can significantly reduce the risk of termination.

Maintaining open communication with your franchisor, staying compliant with operational standards, and meeting your financial and performance obligations are all essential components of safeguarding your business. Additionally, being prepared for renewal and understanding your post-termination obligations can help you plan for the future, whether you intend to continue your franchise relationship or explore new business opportunities.

Ultimately, the key to avoiding franchise termination is to remain diligent, informed, and proactive. By fostering a positive working relationship with your franchisor and addressing issues early, you can protect your investment and ensure the long-term success of your franchise business.

14

FRANCHISE RENEWALS AND EXITS: PLANNING FOR THE FUTURE

Franchise agreements are typically not indefinite; they come with a predefined term, which can range anywhere from 5 to 20 years, depending on the specific franchise. As a franchisee, the expiration of your franchise agreement presents a crucial juncture in your business journey. Whether you plan to renew the franchise agreement and continue operating under the same brand, sell your franchise, or exit the system altogether, how you navigate this stage can significantly impact your future, both financially and professionally.

Franchise **renewal** and **exit** decisions are not something that should be left until the last minute. Franchisees need to approach the end of their franchise term strategically, with a clear understanding of their options and a plan in place. In this chapter, we will explore the various aspects of franchise renewals, the process of exiting the franchise system, and how to prepare for either scenario. By understanding the renewal and exit options available, franchisees can make informed decisions that align with their personal and business goals.

UNDERSTANDING FRANCHISE RENEWALS

The **renewal** of a franchise agreement is an opportunity for both the franchisor and the franchisee to reassess the relationship. A renewal is not automatic; it's subject to the terms of the original franchise agreement, which may require the franchisee to meet certain conditions in order to be eligible for renewal. Additionally, the franchisor may have the right to change the terms of the renewed agreement, which could include adjustments to royalty fees, marketing contributions, territory rights, and operational requirements.

Renewal is an important milestone for franchisees because it signals the next phase of the business. However, it's essential to approach renewal with the same diligence and scrutiny as you did when first signing the franchise agreement. The conditions for renewal, potential changes to the agreement, and the financial implications of continuing under the franchise brand must all be carefully evaluated.

WHEN TO START PREPARING FOR FRANCHISE RENEWAL

Franchisees should begin preparing for renewal well in advance of the agreement's expiration. Many franchise agreements specify a timeline by which the franchisee must notify the franchisor of their intent to renew or not renew the contract. This period can range from 6 to 18 months prior to the expiration date. Missing this deadline could result in losing your right to renew.

Here are some steps to consider when preparing for renewal:

1. REVIEW YOUR FRANCHISE AGREEMENT

The first step in preparing for renewal is to thoroughly review the **renewal provisions** in your franchise agreement. These provisions typically outline:

- The **conditions** you must meet to qualify for renewal (e.g., compliance with operational standards, payment of fees, meeting performance benchmarks).
- The **timeline** for submitting your renewal request.

• Any **fees** associated with renewing the agreement, such as a renewal fee or updated franchise fee.

• **Changes** that may be made to the renewed franchise agreement, such as adjustments to royalties or marketing contributions.

Understanding these terms will give you a clear picture of the requirements you must meet and help you avoid any surprises during the renewal process.

2. Assess Your Business Performance

Before committing to another term as a franchisee, it's important to assess the performance of your franchise. Take a close look at your **financials**, including revenue, profitability, and expenses, to determine whether continuing with the franchise is the right decision for your business. Ask yourself the following questions:

• Has my franchise been **profitable**? What are the trends in revenue and expenses?

• Am I **meeting the performance benchmarks** outlined by the franchisor?

• Is there potential for **growth** in my market, or have I reached a point of market saturation?

• What are the **operational challenges** I've faced, and are there solutions available to address them?

By conducting a thorough evaluation of your business, you'll be better equipped to decide whether renewing the franchise is the best option or if it's time to explore other opportunities.

3. Analyze the Current State of the Franchise System

It's also essential to assess the current state of the **franchise system** as a whole. Franchisors can experience growth, stagnation, or decline over time, and their success (or lack thereof) can have a direct impact on your business. Consider the following factors when evaluating the franchise system:

• Is the franchisor continuing to **innovate** and introduce new products, services, or technology that can help my business grow?

• Has the franchisor **expanded** into new markets, and what impact does this have on my territory or competitive landscape?

• Are other franchisees in the system **thriving**, or are there signs of dissatisfaction or closures?

• Has the franchisor's **brand** maintained its reputation and customer loyalty, or have there been any public relations issues that could affect future growth?

By taking stock of the health of the franchise system, you'll have a better sense of whether it's worth continuing to invest in the brand.

4. Plan for Potential Changes to the Franchise Agreement

When renewing your franchise agreement, it's important to be aware that the **terms of the new agreement** may differ from the original contract. Franchisors may update their agreements over time to reflect changes in the market, legal requirements, or their business strategy. Common changes include:

• **Increased royalty fees** or **marketing contributions**.
• Adjustments to the size or **scope of your territory**.
• New **operational requirements** or performance benchmarks.
• Updated **branding guidelines** or marketing strategies.

While you may not be able to negotiate significant changes to the new agreement, it's important to understand how the updated terms will affect your business. If the new agreement introduces terms that you find unfavorable, you may want to consider alternative options, such as selling your franchise or exiting the system.

How to Renew a Franchise Agreement

Once you've made the decision to renew, the next step is to follow the formal process outlined in your franchise agreement. While the process can vary depending on the franchisor, here are the general steps involved in renewing a franchise agreement:

. . .

1. Notify the Franchisor of Your Intent to Renew

Most franchise agreements require franchisees to provide written notice of their intent to renew the agreement within a specified timeframe (often 6 to 12 months before the agreement's expiration). This notice should be submitted in accordance with the terms of the agreement, which may include sending the notice via certified mail or through a designated online portal.

Failing to submit your renewal notice by the deadline could result in the franchisor refusing to renew the agreement, so it's important to mark this date on your calendar and take action well in advance.

2. Complete the Renewal Application

Many franchisors require franchisees to complete a formal **renewal application** as part of the renewal process. This application may include updated financial information, sales data, and documentation demonstrating your compliance with the franchisor's operational standards.

The franchisor may also conduct a **performance review** or **site inspection** to ensure that your franchise is meeting the brand's expectations. If there are any outstanding issues—such as unpaid fees, customer complaints, or operational deficiencies—these will need to be resolved before the franchisor will approve the renewal.

3. Pay the Renewal Fee

Most franchise agreements require franchisees to pay a **renewal fee** when extending their contract. This fee is often lower than the initial franchise fee, but it can still be a significant expense. The renewal fee helps cover the costs of renewing your license to operate under the franchisor's brand and continuing to receive support from the franchisor.

. . .

4. Review and Sign the New Agreement

Once your renewal application is approved and you've paid the renewal fee, the next step is to **review and sign the new franchise agreement**. As mentioned earlier, the terms of the renewed agreement may differ from your original contract, so it's important to read the new document carefully and consult with a **franchise attorney** if necessary.

Once both parties have signed the new agreement, you are officially renewed and can continue operating your franchise under the terms of the new contract.

Exiting the Franchise System

While some franchisees choose to renew their agreements and continue operating under the franchisor's brand, others may decide that it's time to **exit the franchise system**. Exiting the system can take several forms, including selling the franchise, transferring ownership, or simply allowing the agreement to expire without renewing.

Exiting a franchise is a major decision that requires careful planning, as it can have significant financial and legal implications. Whether you're looking to retire, pursue other business opportunities, or simply move on from the franchise, it's important to approach the exit process strategically.

1. Selling Your Franchise

One of the most common ways to exit a franchise is to **sell the business** to a new owner. Selling your franchise allows you to recoup some of the investment you've made in the business and provides a clean exit from the system.

Steps to Selling a Franchise:

1 **Consult with the Franchisor:** Most franchise agreements include provisions governing the sale or transfer of the franchise. You'll need to notify the franchisor of your intent to sell and follow any procedures outlined in the agreement. The franchisor may also have the right to **approve the buyer** and may require the new owner to meet certain qualifications.

2 VALUATION: BEFORE LISTING YOUR FRANCHISE FOR SALE, IT'S important to determine the **value of your business.** This can be done by consulting with a business broker, franchise consultant, or accountant who specializes in valuing franchises. Factors such as revenue, profitability, market conditions, and brand strength will all play a role in determining the sale price.

3 FINDING A BUYER: ONCE YOU'VE DETERMINED THE VALUE OF YOUR franchise, the next step is to find a buyer. You may choose to work with a **business broker** who specializes in selling franchises, or you can market the business yourself through online listings, industry networks, or by reaching out to potential buyers directly. Keep in mind that the franchisor may also assist with finding a buyer, especially if they have a vested interest in ensuring the new franchisee meets their qualifications.

4 FRANCHISOR APPROVAL: MOST FRANCHISE AGREEMENTS INCLUDE A clause that gives the franchisor the **right of first refusal,** which means they have the option to purchase the franchise themselves before you can sell it to a third party. If the franchisor chooses not to buy the business, they will still need to approve the new owner. The franchisor will likely assess the buyer's financial stability, business experience, and ability to operate within the franchise system.

· · ·

5 TRANSFER PROCESS: AFTER THE FRANCHISOR HAS APPROVED THE SALE, you will need to complete the formal **transfer process**. This includes finalizing the sale agreement with the buyer, transferring the franchise license, and ensuring that any outstanding fees or obligations are settled. The buyer will also need to sign a new franchise agreement with the franchisor.

6 EXIT AND TRANSITION: ONCE THE SALE IS FINALIZED, YOU WILL HAND over the business to the new owner. Some franchise agreements require the outgoing franchisee to assist with the **transition** by training the new owner or providing support for a specified period. After this process is complete, you will officially exit the franchise system.

2. TRANSFERRING OWNERSHIP TO FAMILY OR PARTNERS

Another option for exiting the franchise system is to **transfer ownership** to a family member, business partner, or trusted associate. This option is often chosen by franchisees who want to **keep the business in the family** or ensure continuity for their employees and customers.

Steps for Ownership Transfer:

1 FRANCHISE AGREEMENT REVIEW: AS WITH SELLING A FRANCHISE, THE first step is to review the **transfer provisions** in your franchise agreement. Many agreements require the franchisor's approval for any transfer of ownership, even if the transfer is within the family or to a business partner.

2 APPROVAL PROCESS: THE FRANCHISOR WILL LIKELY REQUIRE THE NEW owner to meet the same **qualifications** as any other buyer. This could include financial vetting, business experience, and a commitment to operating the franchise according to the brand's standards. If the new owner does not meet the franchisor's criteria, they may not approve the transfer.

3 LEGAL DOCUMENTATION: YOU WILL NEED TO WORK WITH AN attorney to draft the **legal documentation** required for the transfer. This includes transferring ownership of the business, assets, and any associated liabilities. The new owner will also need to sign a new franchise agreement with the franchisor.

4 TRAINING AND TRANSITION: IF THE NEW OWNER IS NOT ALREADY familiar with the business, you may be required to provide **training and support** during the transition. This ensures that the new owner is prepared to take over day-to-day operations and comply with the franchisor's standards.

3. ALLOWING THE AGREEMENT TO EXPIRE

If you do not wish to renew the franchise agreement and are not interested in selling or transferring the business, you can simply allow the agreement to **expire.** This is the most straightforward exit option, but it also means that you will no longer have the right to operate under the franchisor's brand or use any of their intellectual property.

KEY CONSIDERATIONS FOR EXPIRING AGREEMENTS:

1 CEASING OPERATIONS: ONCE THE AGREEMENT EXPIRES, YOU WILL NEED to **cease all business operations** under the franchise brand. This includes removing any signage, logos, or branding from your location, as well as discontinuing the use of any proprietary systems, products, or services provided by the franchisor.

2 POST-TERMINATION OBLIGATIONS: MOST FRANCHISE AGREEMENTS include **post-termination obligations** that franchisees must fulfill when the agreement expires. These obligations often include returning proprietary materials, paying any outstanding fees, and adhering to any non-compete clauses that prevent you from opening a similar business in the same area.

3 EXIT STRATEGY: BEFORE ALLOWING THE AGREEMENT TO EXPIRE, IT'S important to have an **exit strategy** in place. Consider how you will wind down the business, notify employees and customers, and settle any remaining financial obligations. Planning ahead will help ensure a smooth exit and protect your financial interests.

4. CLOSING THE FRANCHISE

In some cases, franchisees may decide to simply **close the franchise** and liquidate the business. This is typically the last resort if the business is not performing well or if no buyer can be found. Closing a franchise requires careful planning to minimize losses and meet any legal obligations.

STEPS TO CLOSING A FRANCHISE:

1 NOTIFY THE FRANCHISOR: THE FIRST STEP IN CLOSING YOUR franchise is to notify the franchisor of your intent to close. This should be done in accordance with the terms of the franchise agreement, which may require formal written notice.

. . .

2 SETTLE FINANCIAL OBLIGATIONS: YOU WILL NEED TO SETTLE ANY outstanding fees or debts, including royalties, marketing contributions, and other financial obligations owed to the franchisor. Additionally, you may need to pay **severance** to employees and settle any outstanding contracts or leases.

3 LIQUIDATE ASSETS: DEPENDING ON THE TERMS OF YOUR FRANCHISE agreement, you may be required to **sell or return certain assets** (such as proprietary equipment or signage) to the franchisor. Any remaining assets, such as inventory or equipment, can be sold to recoup some of your investment.

4 HANDLE LEGAL AND TAX MATTERS: CLOSING A BUSINESS INVOLVES A number of legal and tax considerations. You will need to **dissolve the business entity**, file final tax returns, and ensure that all legal requirements for closing a business are met. It's advisable to work with an accountant and attorney to navigate these matters.

5 POST-TERMINATION OBLIGATIONS: AS WITH OTHER EXIT STRATEGIES, you will need to comply with any **post-termination obligations** outlined in the franchise agreement, such as non-compete clauses or the return of proprietary materials.

PLANNING FOR LIFE AFTER THE FRANCHISE

Exiting a franchise system is a major decision that can have a significant impact on your personal and professional life. Whether you are selling your business, transferring ownership, or closing the franchise, it's important to have a clear plan for **life after the franchise.**

• **Financial Planning**: Exiting a franchise can result in a financial windfall (if you sell the business) or financial losses (if you close the business). It's essential to plan for either scenario by consulting with a financial advisor to ensure that you have a strategy for managing your finances after the exit.

- **New Business Opportunities:** Many franchisees who exit the system go on to pursue **new business opportunities**, whether in franchising or independent entrepreneurship. Consider whether you want to explore other franchise opportunities or start a new business outside of the franchising model.

- **Retirement:** For some franchisees, exiting the franchise marks the beginning of **retirement**. If this is your plan, make sure that you have a solid retirement strategy in place, including managing your investments, savings, and income needs.

CONCLUSION: NAVIGATING RENEWALS AND EXITS WITH CONFIDENCE

The decision to renew or exit a franchise is a pivotal moment in your journey as a franchisee. Whether you choose to continue your relationship with the franchisor, sell the business, or pursue new opportunities, it's important to approach this decision with careful planning and a clear understanding of your options.

Renewing a franchise offers the chance to build on the foundation you've established and continue benefiting from the franchisor's support and brand recognition. However, it's essential to evaluate the new terms of the agreement, assess your business performance, and ensure that renewing aligns with your long-term goals.

Exiting the franchise system, whether through a sale, transfer, or closure, requires strategic planning and attention to detail. By following the proper procedures, settling financial obligations, and preparing for the next phase of your career, you can exit the system on your own terms and protect your investment.

Ultimately, whether you renew or exit, the key to success is **proactive planning**. By understanding the renewal and exit processes, preparing well in advance, and seeking professional advice when needed, you can navigate this critical stage with confidence and ensure the best possible outcome for your business and your future.

PART V

LONG-TERM SUCCESS IN FRANCHISING

15

SCALING AND GROWING YOUR FRANCHISE BUSINESS

After you've established a successful franchise location, the natural next step for many franchisees is to consider **scaling** their business. Scaling a franchise means expanding beyond a single location, either by opening additional units or growing the size and capacity of the original location. Whether your goal is to increase profitability, build an empire of franchise units, or diversify your portfolio, growing within a franchise system can be a highly rewarding path. However, scaling comes with its own set of challenges, and success requires strategic planning, effective management, and a deep understanding of both the franchise model and the market in which you operate.

In this chapter, we will explore the key considerations and steps involved in scaling your franchise business. We'll discuss the benefits of multi-unit ownership, the potential pitfalls of rapid expansion, and the strategies you can employ to ensure sustained growth over the long term. Whether you're interested in acquiring additional franchise locations, expanding your existing operation, or exploring new franchise concepts, this chapter will provide a roadmap for scaling your business successfully.

•   •   •

THE BENEFITS OF SCALING A FRANCHISE BUSINESS

Scaling your franchise can offer numerous advantages, both financial and operational. While managing one franchise location can provide a solid income, owning and operating multiple units can significantly increase your profitability and give you greater influence within the franchise system. Here are some of the key benefits of scaling your franchise business:

1. INCREASED REVENUE AND PROFITABILITY

The most obvious benefit of scaling your franchise business is the potential for **increased revenue** and **profitability**. By opening additional franchise units or expanding the capacity of your current location, you can generate more sales and, ultimately, higher profits. For many franchisees, this is the primary motivation behind scaling their business.

- **Economies of Scale:** As you add more locations, you can take advantage of **economies of scale.** This means that your costs per unit (such as purchasing supplies, equipment, or marketing) may decrease because you're buying in bulk or negotiating better rates with vendors. These savings can directly improve your profit margins across all of your locations.

- **Diversification of Revenue Streams:** Scaling allows you to diversify your revenue streams. For example, if one location is underperforming or experiencing a temporary downturn due to local economic conditions, other locations can help offset those losses. This reduces your financial risk and makes your overall business more resilient.

2. INCREASED BRAND PRESENCE AND MARKET SHARE

As you expand your franchise footprint, you also increase your **brand presence** in the market. This not only benefits your individual locations but also contributes to the overall strength of the franchise system. A greater presence in the market can lead to:

• **Higher Customer Awareness**: Opening multiple locations helps to reinforce the brand in the minds of consumers. The more visible your brand is, the more likely customers are to choose it over competitors, especially if they have positive experiences at multiple locations.

• **Dominating Your Territory**: If you're operating within an exclusive territory, opening additional units within that area can help you dominate the market and prevent competitors from gaining a foothold. If your territory is non-exclusive, scaling quickly can help you capture market share before other franchisees or competitors move in.

3. Building Wealth and Equity

Scaling your franchise business can also help you build **long-term wealth** and **equity**. Each new location you open or acquire adds value to your overall business, creating a portfolio of assets that can be sold or transferred in the future. By building a multi-unit operation, you increase the overall value of your business and create a **sellable asset** that can provide significant financial rewards when you eventually exit the system.

• **Franchise Portfolio**: Franchisees who own multiple units often build a **portfolio** of locations that can be sold as a package to an investor or another franchisee. This can result in a higher overall sale price than if you were to sell a single location.

• **Increased Leverage with the Franchisor**: Multi-unit owners typically have greater **influence** within the franchise system, as they represent a larger portion of the franchise's revenue and success. This can provide you with more leverage when negotiating with the franchisor on issues such as royalties, fees, or support.

4. Leadership and Management Development

As you scale your franchise business, you'll need to develop **leadership** and **management skills** to oversee multiple locations. This experience not only helps you grow as a business owner but also positions you for future opportunities, whether within the franchise system or in other ventures.

• **Building a Management Team**: To successfully scale, you'll need to delegate day-to-day responsibilities to a trusted **management team**. This allows you to focus on strategic planning and growth rather than being involved in the minutiae of each location's operations. Developing a strong team is critical to ensuring the success of multiple units.

• **Gaining Business Expertise**: The process of scaling a franchise requires you to develop expertise in areas such as finance, human resources, marketing, and operations. These skills are transferable and can be applied to other businesses or investment opportunities in the future.

THE CHALLENGES OF SCALING A FRANCHISE

While scaling your franchise business offers significant benefits, it also comes with a number of challenges. Expanding too quickly or without the proper infrastructure in place can lead to operational issues, financial strain, and even the failure of the business. Below are some of the most common challenges franchisees face when scaling their operations:

1. MAINTAINING OPERATIONAL CONSISTENCY

One of the biggest challenges in scaling a franchise is maintaining **operational consistency** across multiple locations. Franchisees must ensure that each unit adheres to the franchisor's standards and delivers a consistent experience to customers, regardless of location.

• **Staff Training and Management**: As you open more locations, it becomes increasingly difficult to personally oversee the training and management of staff. You'll need to implement robust **training programs** and hire experienced managers who can maintain the quality of service and operations at each location.

• **Quality Control:** Ensuring **quality control** becomes more complex as you expand. You'll need to establish systems for monitoring performance, customer satisfaction, and compliance with the franchisor's standards across all of your units.

2. Managing Cash Flow and Financing

Scaling a franchise requires a significant investment of time, money, and resources. While the potential for higher revenue is attractive, the upfront costs of expansion can strain your **cash flow** and lead to financial challenges.

• **Initial Investment:** Opening additional units involves substantial upfront costs, including franchise fees, real estate, construction or renovation, equipment, inventory, and staffing. You'll need to secure **financing** for these expenses and ensure that your cash flow can support both the expansion and the ongoing operations of your existing units.

• **Debt Management:** Many franchisees take on **debt** to finance expansion, which can be risky if the new locations don't generate revenue as quickly as expected. It's important to carefully manage your debt load and have a clear plan for repaying loans while maintaining profitability.

3. Balancing Growth with Operational Capacity

Expanding too quickly can lead to **growing pains** if your business doesn't have the operational capacity to support multiple locations. As a multi-unit owner, you'll need to balance your desire for growth with your ability to effectively manage and support each unit.

• **Operational Infrastructure:** Before expanding, ensure that you have the **operational infrastructure** in place to support multiple locations. This includes having a strong management team, reliable supply chain partners, and systems for monitoring performance across all units.

• **Overextending Yourself:** Many franchisees who scale too quickly find themselves **overextended**—juggling too many responsibilities and not having enough time to focus on critical aspects of the business. It's important to delegate tasks and build a team that can handle day-to-day operations so that you can focus on growth and strategy.

4. Maintaining Franchisee-Franchisor Relationships

As you scale, your relationship with the franchisor becomes even more important. Franchisors may have specific requirements or restrictions for multi-unit ownership, and maintaining open lines of communication is key to ensuring a smooth expansion process.

• **Compliance with Franchisor Standards:** As a multi-unit owner, you'll be expected to meet the franchisor's standards across all locations. This may include participating in **franchise advisory councils**, adhering to performance benchmarks, and complying with new policies or initiatives introduced by the franchisor.

• **Negotiating for Better Terms:** Multi-unit owners often have more **leverage** when negotiating with the franchisor, especially if they represent a significant portion of the franchise's revenue. You may be able to negotiate more favorable terms, such as lower royalty rates, larger territories, or additional support from the franchisor.

Key Strategies for Scaling a Franchise Successfully

Scaling a franchise business requires careful planning, strong leadership, and a clear vision for growth. The following strategies can help you navigate the challenges of expansion and ensure long-term success:

1. Develop a Growth Plan

Before embarking on any expansion, it's essential to develop a comprehensive **growth plan** that outlines your objectives, strategies, and timeline for scaling your business. Your growth plan should include:

- **Target Locations:** Identify the **markets** where you plan to expand. Consider factors such as population density, competition, and consumer demand when selecting new locations.

- **Financing Strategy:** Determine how you will **finance** your expansion, whether through loans, personal savings, or reinvesting profits from your existing units.

- **Operational Capacity:** Assess your **operational capacity** to ensure that you have the infrastructure, staff, and resources to support multiple locations.

- **Exit Strategy**

- **Exit Strategy:** While planning for growth, it's also important to consider your **exit strategy**. Whether you plan to eventually sell your entire franchise portfolio, pass it on to family members, or simply operate it as a long-term investment, having a clear exit strategy will help guide your decisions as you expand.

2. Build a Strong Management Team

As you expand, you won't be able to personally oversee every aspect of your business at each location. Therefore, it's critical to build a **strong management team** that can run the day-to-day operations and maintain the standards of your franchise across all units.

- **Hire Experienced Managers:** Look for managers with **experience** in multi-unit operations or in running high-volume businesses. These individuals should have strong leadership skills, the ability to manage teams, and a clear understanding of the franchise system's standards and expectations.

- **Train Your Team:** Develop a comprehensive **training program** that ensures your management team understands the operational procedures, customer service expectations, and brand guidelines set by the franchisor. Ongoing training is also important to keep your team updated on any changes or improvements in the system.

- **Empower Your Managers:** Trust your management team to

make decisions and solve problems at the local level. Empowering them with **decision-making authority** will allow you to focus on strategic growth and long-term planning while ensuring the smooth operation of each unit.

3. STANDARDIZE SYSTEMS AND PROCESSES

One of the keys to successful scaling is the ability to **standardize** systems and processes across all of your locations. This ensures consistency in operations, customer experience, and financial performance.

- **Implement Technology**: Utilize **technology** such as point-of-sale (POS) systems, inventory management software, and customer relationship management (CRM) platforms to streamline operations across all units. Technology allows you to monitor sales, expenses, and performance metrics in real-time, giving you the data you need to make informed decisions.

- **Create Standard Operating Procedures (SOPs)**: While the franchisor will provide certain operational guidelines, you may need to create your own **internal SOPs** to address the specific needs of your multi-unit operation. This could include standardized training materials, customer service protocols, or financial reporting procedures.

- **Monitor Performance**: Regularly review **key performance indicators (KPIs)** across all locations to identify areas of strength and areas that need improvement. Having standardized processes in place will allow you to quickly implement changes and ensure that all units are performing at the highest level.

4. SECURE ADEQUATE FINANCING

Scaling a franchise business requires significant financial investment, so it's essential to secure the necessary **financing** to support your growth. There are several options available for financing your expansion:

- **Traditional Bank Loans:** Many franchisees finance their growth through **traditional bank loans.** These loans can provide the capital needed for upfront expenses such as franchise fees, equipment, real estate, and initial operating costs.

- **Franchise-Specific Lenders:** Some lenders specialize in providing financing to franchisees. These **franchise-specific lenders** may offer more favorable terms, such as lower interest rates or longer repayment periods, as they understand the franchise model and the associated risks.

- **SBA Loans:** The **Small Business Administration (SBA)** offers loan programs designed to help franchisees access financing. SBA loans are often easier to qualify for than traditional loans and may offer lower interest rates and more flexible repayment terms.

- **Reinvesting Profits:** If your existing units are profitable, you may choose to **reinvest profits** into opening new locations. This can reduce your reliance on external financing and allow you to grow your business more sustainably.

5. Expand at a Sustainable Pace

While it may be tempting to open as many units as quickly as possible, rapid expansion can lead to **growing pains** if not done carefully. It's important to scale at a **sustainable pace** that allows you to manage the operational and financial challenges of each new location.

- **Assess Each Location's Performance:** Before opening additional units, ensure that your existing locations are **performing well** and generating enough revenue to support further expansion. If one or more locations are struggling, it's better to address these issues before expanding further.

- **Set Realistic Growth Goals:** Establish **realistic growth goals** that align with your financial capacity, market conditions, and operational infrastructure. Expanding too quickly without the necessary resources can lead to overextension and potential failure.

- **Monitor Market Conditions:** As you expand, keep an eye on

market conditions and **consumer trends** that may affect your business. This will allow you to make informed decisions about where and when to open new locations.

6. Stay Connected with the Franchisor

Maintaining a strong relationship with your franchisor is essential when scaling your franchise business. As a multi-unit owner, you may have more **leverage** and **influence** within the franchise system, but it's still important to work collaboratively with the franchisor.

- **Leverage Franchisor Support:** Many franchisors offer additional support and resources to multi-unit owners, such as marketing assistance, field support, or training programs. Take advantage of these resources to ensure that your expansion is successful.

- **Communicate Regularly:** Keep the lines of communication open with your franchisor, especially when planning new locations or addressing challenges at existing units. Regular communication ensures that both parties are aligned and working toward the same goals.

- **Participate in Franchise Advisory Councils:** If your franchise system has an advisory council, consider joining it. These councils provide multi-unit owners with a platform to share feedback, offer suggestions, and help shape the direction of the franchise system.

Conclusion: Scaling for Long-Term Success

Scaling a franchise business can be one of the most rewarding aspects of being a franchisee, offering the potential for increased profitability, market dominance, and long-term wealth creation. However, successful scaling requires careful planning, effective management, and a strategic approach to growth.

By developing a comprehensive growth plan, building a strong management team, standardizing your operations, securing adequate financing, and expanding at a sustainable pace, you can navigate the challenges of scaling and position your business for long-term success.

Moreover, maintaining open communication with your franchisor and leveraging the resources and support available to multi-unit owners will ensure that you continue to thrive within the franchise system.

Ultimately, the decision to scale your franchise business is a personal one that depends on your goals, financial capacity, and readiness to take on the challenges of expansion. By approaching this decision with the right mindset and the right tools, you can build a thriving franchise empire and achieve your long-term business objectives.

16

BUILDING A MULTI-UNIT FRANCHISE EMPIRE

Once you've successfully opened and operated a single franchise location, the next logical step for many franchisees is to pursue **multi-unit ownership**—the process of expanding from one location to several, and ultimately building an empire of franchise businesses. Multi-unit ownership is one of the most effective ways to scale a business, diversify revenue streams, and increase your influence within the franchise system. However, managing multiple franchise units comes with unique challenges, from operational oversight and leadership to financial management and strategic growth.

In this chapter, we will delve into the intricacies of building a **multi-unit franchise empire.** We will explore the benefits and risks of multi-unit ownership, how to effectively manage multiple locations, and the strategies needed to scale your business sustainably. Whether you're looking to own a handful of locations or envision running a large portfolio of franchises across multiple territories, this chapter will provide the foundation for successfully growing and managing a multi-unit franchise business.

.   .   .

The Rise of Multi-Unit Ownership

Multi-unit ownership has become an increasingly popular strategy in the franchise world. In fact, many franchise systems actively encourage franchisees to own multiple units, as it helps drive growth, maintain brand consistency, and ensure a more stable revenue stream for both the franchisee and franchisor. According to recent industry reports, nearly 54% of all franchise units in the U.S. are owned by multi-unit operators, underscoring the shift toward this model.

Multi-unit franchisees often experience greater **financial success** than single-unit owners because they benefit from economies of scale, operational efficiencies, and increased leverage within the franchise system. By leveraging their expertise and existing infrastructure, multi-unit operators can achieve faster growth and higher profits than if they were managing just one location.

The Benefits of Multi-Unit Franchise Ownership

Expanding from a single location to multiple units offers a range of benefits, from increased revenue and profitability to greater influence within the franchise system. Here are some of the key advantages of multi-unit ownership:

1. Diversification of Revenue Streams

One of the most significant advantages of multi-unit ownership is the **diversification of revenue streams.** Operating multiple franchise locations allows you to spread your financial risk across several units, ensuring that your overall business remains stable even if one location underperforms.

- **Geographic Diversification:** By owning locations in different geographic areas, you can reduce your exposure to localized economic downturns, changes in customer demand, or competitive pressures. For example, if one location experiences a temporary decline in sales due to local competition, other locations in different markets can offset those losses.

• **Consistent Cash Flow:** With multiple units generating revenue, you're more likely to achieve consistent cash flow, even if individual locations have fluctuations in sales. This can provide greater financial security and allow you to reinvest profits into further expansion or other business opportunities.

2. Economies of Scale

As a multi-unit franchise owner, you can take advantage of **economies of scale**, which allows you to reduce costs and improve operational efficiency as you expand.

• **Bulk Purchasing Power:** When you own multiple locations, you can negotiate better deals with suppliers by purchasing in bulk. This can lower your costs for inventory, equipment, and other essential supplies, ultimately improving your profit margins across all units.

• **Shared Resources:** Multi-unit owners can often **share resources** across locations, such as marketing materials, management staff, and technology systems. For example, you may be able to centralize administrative functions such as payroll, bookkeeping, and HR, reducing overhead and freeing up more time for strategic planning.

• **Operational Efficiency:** Owning multiple units allows you to **standardize processes** and optimize operations. By implementing consistent training programs, customer service protocols, and management strategies across all locations, you can streamline operations and improve the efficiency of each unit.

3. Stronger Leverage with the Franchisor

As a multi-unit franchise owner, you wield greater **influence** within the franchise system compared to single-unit operators. Franchisees who own multiple units often generate a significant portion of the franchisor's overall revenue, which can give them more leverage when negotiating fees, royalties, or support.

- **Negotiating Better Terms:** Multi-unit owners are often in a stronger position to negotiate **favorable terms** with the franchisor. This could include lower royalty rates, reduced franchise fees for additional units, or more flexible territory agreements.

- **Increased Support:** Franchisors are typically more invested in the success of multi-unit operators, as their success directly impacts the franchise system's overall performance. As a result, multi-unit franchisees may receive additional support from the franchisor, such as marketing assistance, operational guidance, and field support.

4. GREATER POTENTIAL FOR WEALTH BUILDING

Multi-unit ownership provides greater potential for **wealth building** over the long term. As you expand your portfolio of franchise units, you are creating valuable assets that can be sold or passed down to future generations.

- **Asset Appreciation:** Each franchise unit you own represents an asset that can appreciate in value over time. By building a portfolio of successful franchise locations, you are increasing the overall value of your business, which can result in a substantial financial windfall when you choose to sell.

- **Exit Strategy:** Multi-unit franchisees often have more **exit options** than single-unit owners. You can choose to sell individual units, sell the entire portfolio to another franchisee or investor, or pass the business down to family members. A large portfolio of franchise locations is often more attractive to buyers, as it offers immediate scale and proven profitability.

CHALLENGES OF MULTI-UNIT FRANCHISE OWNERSHIP

While the benefits of multi-unit ownership are significant, there are also several challenges that franchisees must navigate to ensure long-term success. Managing multiple units requires a different skill set than running a single location, and expanding too quickly can lead to operational and financial strain. Here are some of the key challenges of multi-unit ownership:

1. OPERATIONAL OVERSIGHT AND QUALITY CONTROL

Managing multiple franchise units presents a significant challenge in terms of **operational oversight** and maintaining **quality control.** As a multi-unit owner, you won't be able to personally oversee the day-to-day operations at each location, which means you'll need to rely on a strong management team to ensure that each unit operates smoothly and consistently.

• **Delegating Responsibility:** Effective multi-unit ownership requires you to **delegate responsibilities** to trusted managers who can run the daily operations of each location. You'll need to develop leadership and management skills to build a team that can maintain operational standards across all units.

• **Maintaining Consistency:** Ensuring that each location delivers a consistent customer experience is critical to the success of your business. Inconsistent service or quality at one location can harm the reputation of your entire franchise portfolio, so it's important to implement **standardized processes** and conduct regular audits to monitor performance.

2. FINANCIAL MANAGEMENT AND CAPITAL INVESTMENT

Scaling a franchise business requires significant **capital investment** and effective **financial management.** Opening additional units involves upfront costs such as franchise fees, real estate, construction, equipment, and staffing, which can strain your cash flow if not managed carefully.

• **Securing Financing:** As you expand, you may need to secure additional **financing** to cover the costs of opening new locations. This could involve taking out loans, seeking investors, or reinvesting profits from your existing units. Careful financial planning is essential to ensure that you can meet your financial obligations while maintaining profitability.

• **Managing Cash Flow**: With multiple locations, managing **cash flow** becomes more complex. You'll need to carefully monitor the financial performance of each unit and ensure that you have enough working capital to cover expenses across all locations.

3. Human Resources and Staffing

Managing a larger business with multiple locations requires effective **human resources** management and the ability to recruit, train, and retain a high-quality workforce. As a multi-unit owner, you'll need to ensure that each location is staffed with well-trained employees who can deliver consistent service.

• **Recruiting and Retaining Talent**: Finding and retaining talented employees is one of the biggest challenges for multi-unit franchisees. You'll need to develop a recruitment strategy that attracts skilled managers and staff, and you may need to offer competitive compensation packages and opportunities for advancement to retain top talent.

• **Training and Development**: Standardizing your **training programs** across all locations is essential to maintaining quality control and ensuring that employees are properly trained in customer service, operations, and compliance with the franchisor's standards.

• **Staffing Flexibility**: As a multi-unit owner, you'll need to be able to **adjust staffing levels** based on the performance and needs of each location. Some locations may require more staff during peak periods, while others may need to cut back during slow times. Having a flexible staffing model allows you to optimize labor costs and maintain profitability.

4. Strategic Planning and Growth Management

Expanding from one franchise unit to multiple units requires careful **strategic planning** to ensure that growth is sustainable and aligned with your long-term goals. Expanding too quickly without the proper infrastructure in place can lead to operational breakdowns and financial strain.

• **Growth Strategy:** Before expanding, it's important to develop a clear **growth strategy** that outlines your goals, timeline, and target markets. Are you looking to dominate a specific territory, or are you expanding into new regions? Understanding the competitive landscape and market conditions will help you make informed decisions about where and when to open new locations.

• **Balancing Growth with Operational Capacity:** It's important to balance your desire for growth with your ability to effectively manage multiple units. Expanding too quickly can lead to **overextension,** while growing too slowly may result

n missed opportunities. As a multi-unit owner, it's essential to find the right balance between **aggressive expansion** and ensuring that each unit operates efficiently and profitably.

Strategies for Building a Multi-Unit Franchise Empire

Building a successful multi-unit franchise business requires a strategic approach to growth, management, and financial planning. Below are several key strategies to help franchisees scale their business sustainably and effectively:

1. Start Small and Scale Gradually

While the idea of quickly expanding to multiple locations may seem attractive, it's often better to **start small** and scale gradually. Focusing on opening a second or third unit before moving into rapid expansion allows you to fine-tune your operations and management processes, ensuring that each location is successful before taking on additional challenges.

• **Test and Learn:** Use your first few locations to **test** your management strategies, operational efficiencies, and staffing models.

Learning from these early experiences will help you identify areas for improvement, which can be applied to future locations.

• **Plan for Controlled Growth:** Establish a timeline for growth that aligns with your financial resources and operational capacity. Expanding at a controlled pace allows you to maintain quality and ensures that each new location meets the franchisor's performance benchmarks.

2. BUILD A SCALABLE INFRASTRUCTURE

To support long-term growth, it's important to build a **scalable infrastructure** that can accommodate the addition of new locations without overwhelming your existing operations. This involves creating systems, processes, and structures that allow you to efficiently manage multiple units.

• **Centralize Operations:** Consider **centralizing** key operational functions, such as payroll, accounting, and HR, to reduce redundancy and streamline processes. Having a centralized back-office operation can free up time and resources, allowing you to focus on strategic growth.

• **Implement Technology Solutions:** Utilize **technology** to manage operations across multiple units. POS systems, customer relationship management (CRM) software, and employee scheduling tools can help automate processes, improve efficiency, and provide real-time data to monitor performance.

• **Develop a Management Hierarchy:** As you expand, you'll need to delegate responsibilities to a team of managers and supervisors who can oversee the day-to-day operations at each location. Establish a clear **management hierarchy**, with district or regional managers responsible for overseeing several units and reporting directly to you.

3. LEVERAGE THE POWER OF MULTI-UNIT FRANCHISING

Many franchisors actively encourage multi-unit ownership, offering special incentives or development programs to franchisees who commit to opening multiple locations. These **multi-unit franchise agreements** provide franchisees with a roadmap for growth and often come with benefits that single-unit franchisees do not receive.

• **Area Development Agreements:** Some franchisors offer **area development agreements (ADAs)**, which give franchisees the exclusive right to develop multiple units within a specific territory over a set period. These agreements often come with reduced franchise fees for each additional location, allowing franchisees to expand at a lower cost.

• **Master Franchise or Regional Developer Roles:** In some cases, franchisors offer **master franchise** or **regional developer** opportunities, where franchisees are responsible for overseeing the development and support of other franchisees within a designated territory. These roles allow franchisees to expand their influence and generate additional revenue through franchise sales and support.

4. Focus on Leadership and Team Development

As a multi-unit franchise owner, you'll need to develop strong **leadership** and **team-building** skills to manage a larger workforce and ensure consistent performance across all units. Building a high-performing management team is critical to scaling your business successfully.

• **Hire the Right People:** Surround yourself with experienced, capable managers who can help you run the business. Hiring the right people is essential, especially when you are overseeing multiple locations. Look for individuals with leadership experience, operational expertise, and the ability to manage teams effectively.

• **Train and Empower Your Team:** Invest in ongoing **training** and development for your managers and staff. Empower them to make decisions, solve problems, and take ownership of their locations. Delegating authority to trusted managers allows you to focus on strategic growth while ensuring that each location runs smoothly.

• **Create a Culture of Accountability:** Establish a **culture of** accountability where managers and employees are responsible for their performance. Set clear expectations, regularly review performance metrics, and reward individuals who meet or exceed goals.

5. Monitor Performance and Adapt

As your franchise portfolio grows, it becomes increasingly important to **monitor performance** across all units and make data-driven decisions. Tracking key performance indicators (KPIs) such as sales, labor costs, customer satisfaction, and operational efficiency will help you identify areas for improvement and capitalize on growth opportunities.

• **Use Data to Drive Decisions:** Leverage technology to collect and analyze performance data in real time. By tracking KPIs across all locations, you can quickly identify trends, spot underperforming units, and make adjustments to improve operations.

• **Adapt to Market Changes:** The market is constantly evolving, and successful multi-unit franchise owners are those who can **adapt** to changes in consumer behavior, competition, and economic conditions. Stay informed about industry trends, and be willing to make adjustments to your business strategy as needed.

6. Maintain Strong Relationships with the Franchisor

Building and maintaining a strong relationship with your franchisor is critical to the success of your multi-unit franchise empire. The franchisor plays a key role in providing support, resources, and guidance as you scale your business.

• **Communicate Regularly:** Stay in regular contact with your franchisor, sharing updates on your growth plans, challenges, and successes. Open communication helps foster a positive working relationship and ensures that you receive the support you need.

• **Participate in Franchise Events:** Attend **franchise conferences**, training sessions, and advisory meetings to stay connected with the franchisor and other franchisees. These events provide valuable networking opportunities and allow you to stay up to date on system-wide initiatives and changes.

Conclusion: Building a Sustainable Multi-Unit Franchise Business

Building a multi-unit franchise empire offers enormous potential for financial success, wealth creation, and personal growth. However, it also requires careful planning, effective management, and a deep understanding of the unique challenges that come with scaling a business.

By starting small, building a scalable infrastructure, and focusing on leadership development, you can lay the foundation for long-term success. Additionally, leveraging multi-unit franchise agreements, monitoring performance, and maintaining strong relationships with your franchisor will position you for sustained growth and profitability.

The journey from single-unit franchisee to multi-unit empire builder requires commitment, resilience, and strategic vision. But for those who approach the challenge with the right mindset and resources, the rewards of building a multi-unit franchise business can be immense—both financially and professionally.

17

FRANCHISE LEADERSHIP: BECOMING A SUCCESSFUL LEADER AND MENTOR

As a franchisee, leadership is an essential skill that drives not only your personal success but also the success of your team and, by extension, your franchise locations. Whether you are managing one location or a multi-unit franchise empire, your ability to lead, inspire, and mentor your employees will determine the overall performance of your business. In a franchise system, leadership goes beyond simply managing daily operations; it involves creating a strong company culture, fostering teamwork, ensuring high standards of service, and mentoring future leaders within your organization.

In this chapter, we will explore the core principles of **franchise leadership** and how you can develop the leadership skills necessary to build a successful and thriving business. We will examine the different leadership styles, how to manage and motivate your team, the role of mentorship in franchise success, and strategies for creating a strong, values-driven culture. Whether you are a first-time franchisee or an experienced multi-unit owner, understanding how to be an effective leader will enable you to maximize the potential of your franchise and set the stage for long-term growth.

· · ·

THE IMPORTANCE OF LEADERSHIP IN FRANCHISING

Leadership is not just about making decisions or giving orders; it's about inspiring others to achieve their best and driving the success of the business through effective communication, motivation, and vision. As a franchisee, you are the **face of the business** at the local level, and your employees look to you for guidance, support, and direction. Effective leadership ensures that your team is motivated, your customers are satisfied, and your business is operating at peak efficiency.

Some key aspects of leadership in a franchise setting include:

• **Establishing a Strong Company Culture:** Your leadership sets the tone for the work environment. A positive, values-driven culture leads to better employee satisfaction, reduced turnover, and higher levels of customer service.

• **Managing Employee Performance:** As a leader, you must be able to manage and improve employee performance through clear expectations, regular feedback, and constructive coaching.

• **Driving Business Growth:** Leadership also involves setting a clear **vision** for the future and making strategic decisions that drive the growth and profitability of your franchise.

• **Ensuring Brand Consistency:** In a franchise system, leadership is critical in ensuring that the brand's standards are consistently upheld across all locations. This requires effective training, monitoring, and enforcement of the franchisor's guidelines.

LEADERSHIP STYLES IN FRANCHISING

There is no one-size-fits-all approach to leadership, and different situations may call for different leadership styles. Understanding your own leadership style—and knowing when to adapt it—can have a significant impact on your business's success. Below are some common leadership styles that franchise owners often adopt, along with their benefits and potential drawbacks.

· · ·

1. The Visionary Leader

Visionary leaders focus on the big picture and are skilled at setting long-term goals and inspiring their teams to work toward a common vision. This leadership style is particularly effective in franchise settings because it helps align the team with the broader objectives of the business and fosters a sense of purpose.

- **Benefits:** Visionary leaders excel at creating **buy-in** among employees by communicating a compelling vision of the future. This style encourages innovation, forward-thinking, and a long-term focus.

- **Drawbacks:** While visionary leadership is great for setting goals, it may sometimes overlook the **details** of day-to-day operations. Leaders who focus too much on the future may miss important operational issues that need immediate attention.

2. The Democratic Leader

Democratic leaders are known for involving their team members in decision-making processes. They value collaboration and seek input from employees before making key decisions. This leadership style is effective for fostering teamwork and ensuring that employees feel valued and empowered.

- **Benefits:** Democratic leadership creates a **collaborative environment** where employees feel invested in the success of the business. It often leads to higher job satisfaction, as employees feel their opinions are valued.

- **Drawbacks:** In situations that require quick decisions, a democratic leadership style can slow down the process. Too much emphasis on consensus can lead to delays or indecision.

3. The Coaching Leader

A **coaching leader** takes a hands-on approach to developing their employees by focusing on their individual strengths and helping them improve in areas where they need growth. This leadership style emphasizes personal and professional development, making it particularly effective in franchise settings where training and skill-building are critical.

- **Benefits:** Coaching leadership helps create **future leaders** within the organization. It fosters a culture of continuous learning and improvement, which can lead to long-term success.

- **Drawbacks:** Coaching takes time, and in high-pressure environments, it may be difficult to dedicate the necessary time to individual development. Additionally, some employees may be resistant to coaching if they are not open to feedback.

4. THE TRANSACTIONAL LEADER

Transactional leaders focus on structure, rules, and performance metrics. They set clear expectations for employees and use rewards and penalties to ensure compliance and achieve specific outcomes. In franchise settings, transactional leadership can be effective for maintaining **consistency** and **standardization**, which are critical to upholding the brand's reputation.

- **Benefits:** This leadership style is great for maintaining **operational efficiency** and ensuring that employees follow established procedures. It is particularly useful in franchises that require strict adherence to brand guidelines, such as food service or retail.

- **Drawbacks:** Transactional leadership can feel rigid and **impersonal**, which may lead to disengagement or low morale among employees. It also tends to focus more on immediate results rather than long-term development or creativity.

5. THE SERVANT LEADER

Servant leaders prioritize the needs of their employees and focus on providing the tools, resources, and support that employees need to succeed. This leadership style is highly empathetic and values the well-being of the team above all else.

- **Benefits:** Servant leadership creates a **positive, supportive** work environment, which can lead to high employee retention, loyalty, and job satisfaction. Employees often feel more motivated to go above and beyond when they know their leader is invested in their well-being.

- **Drawbacks:** Servant leaders may sometimes put the needs of their employees ahead of the needs of the business, which can result in challenges when tough decisions need to be made. Balancing empathy with business objectives is critical for servant leaders.

CREATING A POSITIVE AND PRODUCTIVE FRANCHISE CULTURE

As a franchise leader, one of your most important responsibilities is to create and foster a **positive company culture** that aligns with the values of the franchisor and promotes high performance. A strong company culture not only leads to better employee satisfaction and retention but also translates into higher levels of customer satisfaction, as employees are more likely to provide excellent service when they are engaged and motivated.

1. DEFINE YOUR CORE VALUES

At the heart of any successful company culture are clearly defined **core values** that guide the behavior of the team and inform decision-making. As a franchisee, you should take the time to establish the values that are most important to your business and communicate them to your employees.

- **Align with the Franchisor's Brand:** While it's important to develop your own values, make sure they align with the overall brand values of the franchisor. This ensures consistency across the franchise system and strengthens the customer's trust in the brand.

- **Incorporate Values into Daily Operations:** Your values should not just be words on a wall—they should be **incorporated into everyday actions.** This means leading by

. . .

2. Build a Collaborative Work Environment

A positive and productive work culture thrives on **collaboration** and open communication. As a franchise leader, it's important to create an environment where employees feel comfortable sharing their ideas, asking questions, and providing feedback. Encouraging open dialogue promotes innovation, helps identify problems early, and fosters a sense of teamwork.

• **Encourage Open Communication:** Regularly solicit feedback from your team through formal meetings, one-on-one discussions, or anonymous surveys. Make sure employees know that their opinions matter and that they have a direct impact on the success of the business.

• **Create Team-Building Opportunities:** Organize team-building activities that allow your employees to develop stronger relationships and work better together. These could range from simple social gatherings to more structured workshops designed to improve collaboration and problem-solving.

3. Recognize and Reward Employees

Recognition is a powerful motivator, and employees who feel valued for their contributions are more likely to stay engaged and perform at their best. In a franchise setting, where consistency and operational efficiency are key, it's important to acknowledge employees who go above and beyond to meet the franchisor's standards or contribute to the growth of the business.

• **Implement an Employee Recognition Program:** Create a formal recognition program that rewards employees for outstanding performance. This could include "Employee of the Month" awards, bonuses for hitting specific performance targets, or public recognition during team meetings.

• **Celebrate Milestones and Achievements:** In addition to recognizing individual accomplishments, make it a point to celebrate team milestones, such as achieving sales goals, launching a new product, or receiving positive customer reviews. Celebrating successes helps reinforce a positive culture and motivates employees to continue striving for excellence.

4. PROVIDE GROWTH AND DEVELOPMENT OPPORTUNITIES

Employees are more likely to stay with your franchise and perform at a high level if they feel they have opportunities for **growth and development**. As a leader, it's important to invest in your employees' personal and professional growth, whether through training, mentorship, or opportunities for advancement.

- **Offer Ongoing Training:** Provide your team with ongoing training opportunities that allow them to develop new skills and improve their performance. This could include on-the-job training, workshops, or even sending employees to franchisor-led training programs.

- **Promote from Within:** Whenever possible, promote employees from within your organization. This not only motivates your team by showing them that there are advancement opportunities, but it also helps you retain institutional knowledge and create a sense of loyalty among your staff.

- **Mentorship:** Establish a mentorship program where experienced employees or managers mentor newer team members. This helps new hires acclimate to the company culture and feel supported as they grow in their roles.

THE ROLE OF MENTORSHIP IN FRANCHISE LEADERSHIP

Mentorship is a key component of leadership, particularly in franchising, where there are opportunities to guide and develop the next generation of leaders within your organization. As a franchise leader, mentoring your managers and employees can help them improve their skills, increase job satisfaction, and prepare for future roles in the company.

. . .

1. Mentor Your Managers

If you are a multi-unit franchise owner, you'll rely heavily on your **managers** to run the day-to-day operations of each location. By mentoring your managers, you can help them develop the skills they need to succeed in their roles and ensure that they are aligned with your vision for the business.

- **Lead by Example:** Demonstrate the leadership qualities you want your managers to emulate, whether it's in decision-making, communication, or how you handle challenges. Managers who see their leaders in action are more likely to adopt those behaviors in their own roles.

- **Provide Regular Feedback:** Give your managers regular, constructive feedback on their performance. Help them identify areas for improvement and provide the tools or resources they need to succeed. Over time, this feedback helps your managers grow into stronger, more effective leaders.

- **Involve Them in Strategic Planning:** Involve your managers in the strategic planning process for your business, whether it's setting sales goals, implementing new initiatives, or making key decisions about operations. This helps them understand the bigger picture and gives them a sense of ownership in the success of the franchise.

2. Develop Future Leaders

Beyond your current management team, it's important to identify and develop **future leaders** within your organization. By investing in the development of high-potential employees, you can create a pipeline of talent that will be ready to step into leadership roles as your business grows.

- **Identify High-Potential Employees:** Look for employees who demonstrate leadership potential, whether through their work ethic, problem-solving abilities, or natural ability to motivate others. These employees can be groomed for future management positions.

- **Offer Leadership Development Programs:** Implement leadership development programs that provide training in areas such as communication, conflict resolution, and decision-making. These programs can help high-potential employees build the skills they need to transition into leadership roles.

- **Create Growth Paths:** Develop clear **career paths** for employees who are interested in leadership roles. By showing them how they can progress within the organization, you motivate them to stay with the company and work toward their career goals.

MAINTAINING LEADERSHIP IN A GROWING FRANCHISE

As your franchise business grows—whether through the addition of more units or an increase in employee headcount—your leadership role will evolve. You will need to shift from hands-on management to more strategic leadership, empowering your managers to take on greater responsibility while you focus on the broader direction of the business.

1. DELEGATE EFFECTIVELY

As your franchise grows, it's important to learn how to **delegate** effectively. While it can be tempting to stay involved in every aspect of the business, trying to manage everything yourself will limit your ability to focus on growth and strategy.

- **Empower Your Team:** Trust your managers and employees to handle the day-to-day operations of each location. Provide them with the resources and training they need to succeed, and empower them to make decisions without your constant oversight.

- **Set Clear Expectations:** When delegating tasks, set clear expectations for what needs to be done, along with deadlines and performance metrics. Ensure that your team understands their responsibilities and how their work contributes to the overall success of the business.

2. FOCUS ON STRATEGIC LEADERSHIP

As your business grows, your role will increasingly shift from tactical, hands-on management to **strategic leadership.** Rather than being involved in the minutiae of daily operations, your focus should be on long-term growth, financial planning, and ensuring that your franchise is positioned for success in the future.

• **Set Long-Term Goals:** Work with your leadership team to set clear, **long-term goals** for your business. These goals should align with both your personal vision and the objectives of the franchisor. Regularly review these goals and adjust them as needed based on market conditions and business performance.

• **Adapt to Changing Conditions:** Franchise businesses operate in dynamic markets, so it's important to remain **adaptable.** Stay informed about industry trends, changes in consumer behavior, and new franchisor initiatives. Use this information to adjust your strategy and ensure that your franchise remains competitive.

Conclusion: Leading for Long-Term Success

Leadership in a franchise business goes far beyond day-to-day management. It's about setting a vision, fostering a positive company culture, developing your team, and driving the long-term success of your business. Whether you're managing a single location or a multi-unit operation, effective leadership is the foundation that allows your franchise to thrive.

By adopting the right leadership style, building a strong team, fostering collaboration, and mentoring future leaders, you can create a franchise business that not only meets but exceeds its potential. Leadership is a continuous journey of learning, adapting, and growing alongside your business—and as you become a stronger leader, you'll position your franchise for sustained success well into the future.

PART VI

THE FUTURE OF FRANCHISING: EMERGING TRENDS AND LEGAL CONSIDERATIONS

18

___

TECHNOLOGY AND FRANCHISING

How Technology Fees and Digital Platforms Are Reshaping Franchising
In recent years, the rapid evolution of technology has transformed nearly every industry, and franchising is no exception. Technology plays a pivotal role in enhancing operational efficiency, improving customer engagement, and driving revenue. At the heart of this transformation are technology fees, which franchisors increasingly require to maintain, support, and develop digital platforms and tools for their franchisees.

TECHNOLOGY FEES

Technology fees have become common in franchise agreements as brands incorporate sophisticated software, e-commerce platforms, and mobile applications into their business models. These fees typically cover a wide range of technology-related services, including:

• **Point of Sale (POS) systems:** Franchisors often provide standardized POS systems that streamline inventory management, sales tracking, and customer data collection.

• **Customer Relationship Management (CRM) systems:** CRM

tools help franchisees manage relationships with customers, automate marketing campaigns, and analyze consumer behavior.

- **Mobile apps and loyalty programs:** Many franchisors provide apps that allow franchisees to engage with customers through loyalty programs, online ordering, and personalized marketing offers.
- **E-commerce platforms:** The rise of online shopping has pushed franchisors to develop integrated e-commerce solutions, allowing franchisees to sell products online in a seamless, branded manner.
- **Digital marketing tools:** Franchisors often provide franchisees with tools for social media marketing, search engine optimization (SEO), and online advertising campaigns.

Technology fees are often structured as a fixed monthly or annual charge, or they may be tied to a percentage of gross sales. While these fees can significantly benefit franchisees by providing access to cutting-edge tools, they can also be a point of contention, particularly when the costs rise without a clear return on investment. Franchisees may question the value of certain technologies or feel that they lack control over which systems they are required to use.

DIGITAL PLATFORMS

Digital platforms have also reshaped the way franchising operates by providing a centralized hub for communication, training, and support. These platforms can offer:

- **Franchisee support portals:** Many franchisors maintain digital platforms where franchisees can access resources like training materials, manuals, marketing assets, and operational guidelines.
- **Training modules:** With the rise of online learning, franchisors increasingly offer digital training programs that allow franchisees and their employees to complete required certifications and skills development courses from anywhere.
- **Data analytics:** Franchisors can provide franchisees with detailed reports and analytics on sales trends, customer demographics, and market performance through digital dashboards.

These digital platforms help standardize operations, reduce costs, and ensure that franchisees are following brand guidelines. However, as these platforms become more critical to daily operations, franchisees often bear the financial responsibility for their maintenance and upgrades through the technology fees outlined above.

Legal Concerns with Technology Usage: Data Privacy and Cybersecurity

The growing reliance on technology in franchising has introduced new legal challenges, particularly concerning data privacy and cybersecurity. Both franchisors and franchisees must comply with evolving legal standards and regulations that protect sensitive customer and business data. These issues have gained significant attention as high-profile data breaches and increasing cyber threats make headlines.

Data Privacy

Franchise systems collect vast amounts of data on customers, including payment information, purchase history, and personal preferences. This data can be used to enhance customer experiences through personalized marketing and loyalty programs, but it also raises significant data privacy concerns. Regulations such as the General Data Protection Regulation (GDPR) in Europe and the California Consumer Privacy Act (CCPA) in the U.S. have created strict requirements for businesses handling personal data.

Franchisors and franchisees must ensure that they:

• **Obtain proper consent** before collecting and processing customer data.

• **Implement transparent data practices,** such as providing clear privacy notices and giving customers the right to access or delete their data.

• **Adopt secure data handling protocols,** including encryption and anonymization, to protect sensitive information.

Franchise agreements should explicitly outline the responsibilities of both franchisors and franchisees regarding data collection, storage, and sharing. Franchisees must ensure that the technology platforms they are required to use comply with applicable privacy regulations, while franchisors must provide guidance and support to help franchisees navigate these legal obligations.

Cybersecurity

In addition to privacy concerns, the rise of digital platforms has created new risks in the form of cybersecurity threats. Franchise networks are particularly vulnerable because of their decentralized nature—each franchisee operates as an independent business but relies on shared technology systems. A cybersecurity breach at one franchise location can compromise the entire brand.

Common cybersecurity risks in franchising include:

• **Data breaches**: Hackers can gain access to customer information or proprietary business data through weak security measures.

• **Ransomware attacks**: Cybercriminals may hold a franchisee's data hostage in exchange for a ransom, disrupting operations and causing financial losses.

• **Phishing scams**: Franchisees and their employees may fall victim to fraudulent emails or websites designed to steal login credentials or sensitive information.

To mitigate these risks, franchisors should implement robust cybersecurity protocols, including regular system updates, firewalls, antivirus software, and employee training on recognizing phishing attacks. Franchise agreements should also address cybersecurity obligations, requiring franchisees to maintain adequate security measures and report any breaches promptly.

Trends in E-Commerce and Their Impact on Franchise Models

The explosive growth of e-commerce has significantly impacted the traditional franchise model. As consumers increasingly turn to online shopping, franchise systems must adapt to this shift in purchasing behavior. E-commerce is no longer an optional aspect of business for many franchise networks—it is a crucial element that shapes how franchisees operate.

Online Sales and Local Markets

One of the key challenges for franchisors in the e-commerce space is balancing the benefits of online sales with the rights of individual franchisees in their local territories. Franchisees may feel that online sales by the franchisor undermine their brick-and-mortar operations, particularly if the franchisor retains a portion of the revenue from online transactions.

To address this concern, franchisors often:

• **Allocate online sales revenue** based on geographic territory, ensuring that local franchisees benefit from e-commerce activity within their regions.

• **Offer click-and-collect services,** where customers order online but pick up their purchases at local franchise locations, driving foot traffic and increasing in-store sales.

• **Develop hybrid models,** where franchisees are given the opportunity to manage their own online sales channels within the franchisor's broader e-commerce platform.

Omnichannel Experiences

Consumers today expect a seamless shopping experience across both physical and digital channels. As a result, franchise systems are embracing **omnichannel strategies** that integrate in-store and online interactions. This approach allows franchisees to meet customer demands for convenience while still maintaining a strong local presence.

Examples of omnichannel initiatives in franchising include:

• **Buy online, pick up in-store (BOPIS):** Franchisees benefit from offering customers the ability to order products online and collect them at their local store.

• **Curbside pickup:** To accommodate customers seeking contactless shopping options, many franchisees now offer curbside pickup for online orders.

• **Mobile ordering:** Apps that enable customers to order ahead for in-store pickup or delivery have become a staple in industries such as food service and retail franchising.

Subscription Models and Membership Programs

Another trend reshaping the franchise landscape is the rise of subscription models and membership programs. Some franchisors are offering subscription-based services, where customers pay a recurring fee in exchange for regular product deliveries or exclusive benefits. This model can drive consistent revenue for franchisees while also fostering customer loyalty.

Conclusion

As technology continues to reshape the franchise industry, both franchisors and franchisees must navigate new opportunities and challenges. Technology fees and digital platforms can provide significant benefits, but they also introduce concerns related to cost, control, and legal compliance. Data privacy and cybersecurity have emerged as critical legal considerations, with evolving regulations and increased cyber threats demanding attention. Finally, the rise of e-commerce and omnichannel experiences is transforming traditional franchise models, requiring brands to adapt to shifting consumer expectations.

In this rapidly changing environment, the most successful franchise systems will be those that embrace technology while maintaining a balance between innovation and operational sustainability. By doing so, they can continue to thrive in an increasingly digital world.

19

INTERNATIONAL FRANCHISING
THE LEGAL CHALLENGES OF EXPANDING A FRANCHISE ABROAD

The Legal Challenges of Expanding a Franchise Abroad

EXPANDING A FRANCHISE INTERNATIONALLY PRESENTS EXCITING opportunities for growth, increased brand visibility, and access to new markets. However, entering foreign markets also brings a host of legal challenges. Franchisors must navigate the complexities of international law, differing business practices, and cultural expectations—all of which can significantly impact the success of a cross-border expansion.

Franchising abroad requires careful planning and a deep understanding of the legal framework in the target country. While the basic structure of a franchise agreement may remain the same, international franchising introduces several new elements, including compliance with foreign laws, currency exchange, language barriers, and the protection of intellectual property.

Common Legal Challenges in International Franchising

. . .

1 REGULATORY AND COMPLIANCE REQUIREMENTS

Each country has its own set of rules governing franchises. Some countries have well-established franchise laws that mirror those in the franchisor's home country, while others may have little or no regulation. Regardless, franchisors must comply with local laws that often govern:

○ **Disclosure requirements:** Many countries require franchisors to provide detailed disclosure documents to prospective franchisees. These documents may need to be translated into the local language and tailored to meet local legal standards.

○ **Registration of franchise agreements:** In some jurisdictions, franchisors must register their franchise agreements with local authorities before they can begin operations. This can add significant time and complexity to the expansion process.

○ **Taxation:** International franchises are subject to both local and international tax laws, which can affect royalties, fees, and profits. Understanding the tax implications of franchising in a foreign market is crucial for avoiding penalties and maximizing profitability.

○ **Employment laws:** Labor laws vary greatly between countries. Franchisors need to ensure that their franchisees comply with local employment laws regarding wages, working conditions, and employee rights.

2 INTELLECTUAL PROPERTY PROTECTION

Protecting intellectual property (IP) is a critical concern in international franchising. A franchisor's brand, trademarks, and proprietary systems are the backbone of its business model, and ensuring that these are safeguarded in a foreign country is essential.

○ **Trademark registration:** Franchisors must register their trademarks in each country where they operate. In some jurisdictions, trademark protection is granted on a "first-to-file" basis, meaning that if the franchisor does not register the trademark early, a third party may do so, potentially blocking the franchisor's use of its own brand.

○ **Copyright and trade secret protections:** Franchisors need to ensure that their training materials, operational manuals, and proprietary business processes are protected under local copyright and trade secret laws.

3 Currency and Financial Considerations

Operating in foreign markets often involves dealing with multiple currencies. Franchisors must consider:

○ **Exchange rates:** Fluctuating currency exchange rates can impact profitability, especially when royalties and fees are calculated in the franchisor's home currency but collected in the local currency.

○ **Repatriation of profits:** Some countries have restrictions on how profits can be transferred out of the country. Franchisors need to understand these restrictions and plan accordingly to avoid complications.

4 Dispute Resolution

Disputes are inevitable in any business relationship, but international franchising adds an extra layer of complexity when it comes to resolving them. Franchisors must decide how disputes with international franchisees will be handled, including:

○ **Jurisdiction:** Franchise agreements must specify which country's courts will have jurisdiction over disputes. Without clear provisions, a franchisor could find itself litigating in an unfamiliar legal system.

○ **Arbitration clauses:** Many international franchise agreements include arbitration clauses, which provide an alternative to litigation. However, franchisors must ensure that the arbitration process is enforceable in the target country.

Key Differences in International Franchise Laws and Agreements

. . .

WHILE MANY CORE PRINCIPLES OF FRANCHISING REMAIN CONSISTENT across borders, the legal landscape can vary significantly from country to country. Franchisors expanding internationally must be aware of key differences in franchise laws and agreement structures that could impact their operations.

1. DISCLOSURE REQUIREMENTS

In the United States, franchisors are required to provide a Franchise Disclosure Document (FDD) to prospective franchisees. This document contains detailed information about the franchisor's business, including financial statements, litigation history, and obligations of the franchisee. Many other countries, such as Canada and Australia, have similar disclosure requirements. However, the specific content and timing of these disclosures can vary.

For example:

• **France:** Franchisors must provide a pre-contractual disclosure document, called the "Document d'Information Précontractuelle" (DIP), at least 20 days before the franchise agreement is signed.

• **Brazil:** Brazilian law requires a disclosure document to be delivered at least 10 days before signing the franchise agreement. It must include information such as the franchisor's history, financial status, and litigation involving the franchise.

Failure to comply with disclosure requirements can result in penalties, voided contracts, or even lawsuits.

2. REGISTRATION OF FRANCHISE AGREEMENTS

In some countries, franchisors must register their franchise agreements with local regulatory bodies. This process often involves submitting the agreement for review to ensure it complies with local laws.

• **China:** China's franchise laws require franchisors to have operated at least two franchise units for one year before registering their franchise with the Ministry of Commerce.

- **Malaysia:** Franchise agreements must be registered with the Registrar of Franchises, and franchisors must provide annual financial reports and franchisee details to the government.

3. Royalty Payments and Fees

Royalty structures and fees may differ in international franchise agreements due to varying tax and business regulations. Franchisors must determine whether their typical royalty model—such as a percentage of gross sales—can be applied in the target country or if adjustments are necessary.

Some countries impose taxes on royalties paid to foreign entities, which can reduce the profitability of a franchisee. In such cases, franchisors may need to work with local tax experts to create a structure that minimizes the tax burden.

4. Intellectual Property Laws

As mentioned earlier, IP protection laws can vary significantly between countries. In some countries, enforcing IP rights may be more challenging due to weak legal systems or inconsistent enforcement of trademark or copyright protections.

For example:

- **India:** While India has robust IP laws on paper, enforcement can be slow, and court systems may be backlogged. Franchisors need to be proactive in registering their trademarks and monitoring for infringement.

- **Mexico:** Mexico follows a "first-to-file" system for trademark registration, which makes it important for franchisors to secure trademark protections early, even before they begin operations.

Tips for Navigating Cross-Border Franchise Relationships

Given the complexity of international franchising, franchisors must take proactive steps to navigate cross-border relationships successfully. Below are some key tips for managing international franchise relationships.

1. Work with Local Experts

One of the most critical steps a franchisor can take when expanding abroad is partnering with local experts. This includes:

- **Legal counsel:** Engage legal counsel with expertise in the franchise laws of the target country to ensure compliance with local regulations.

- **Tax advisors:** Work with tax professionals who understand the international tax landscape and can help optimize your franchise's financial structure.

- **Market consultants:** Hire local market experts who understand the cultural nuances and business practices of the target country, which can impact everything from marketing strategies to customer service expectations.

2. Tailor the Franchise Agreement

Franchisors should not assume that their domestic franchise agreement will be suitable for international use. Tailoring the agreement to the legal and business environment of each country is essential. This includes:

- **Modifying royalty and fee structures** to account for local taxation and economic conditions.

- **Incorporating local dispute resolution mechanisms,** such as arbitration panels or courts familiar with local laws.

- **Addressing local employment laws** in the agreement, including provisions for how franchisees must comply with local labor standards.

3. Protect Intellectual Property Early

Before entering a new market, franchisors should register their trademarks, copyrights, and patents in the target country. This is particularly important in countries with a "first-to-file" system, where a delay could result in another party securing rights to the franchisor's intellectual property.

Franchisors should also actively monitor their IP for any infringement and be prepared to enforce their rights through local legal channels when necessary.

4. Provide Comprehensive Training and Support

Cross-border franchises often face operational challenges due to cultural differences, language barriers, and unfamiliar business practices. Franchisors can mitigate these challenges by providing comprehensive training and ongoing support to international franchisees. This may include:

- **Localized training programs:** Tailor training materials to address the specific challenges and opportunities of the local market.
- **Cultural training:** Ensure that franchisees understand the brand's values while also being sensitive to local customs and consumer behavior.

5. Be Flexible and Patient

International franchising requires flexibility and patience. Success may not come as quickly as it does in domestic markets, and franchisors must be prepared to adjust their strategies in response to local market conditions. Building strong relationships with international franchisees and remaining open to feedback can help franchisors navigate the complexities of cross-border expansion.

Conclusion

Expanding a franchise internationally presents significant opportunities, but it also requires careful planning and a deep understanding of the legal and business environment in the target country.

From navigating complex regulatory requirements to protecting intellectual property, franchisors must address a wide range of challenges to ensure a successful expansion. By working with local experts, tailoring franchise agreements, and providing comprehensive support, franchisors can overcome these challenges and build successful international franchises.

20

____

NEW LEGAL TRENDS IN FRANCHISING

THE IMPACT OF RECENT LEGISLATION ON FRANCHISE RELATIONSHIPS

Franchising is a dynamic and evolving business model, and recent legislative developments have begun reshaping the legal landscape for both franchisors and franchisees. The introduction of new laws and regulations across various jurisdictions has significant implications for the franchise industry, altering how franchise relationships are structured and governed.

I. JOINT EMPLOYER LIABILITY

One of the most significant legal developments in recent years is the ongoing debate over **joint employer liability**. This issue revolves around whether franchisors can be held responsible for the actions of their franchisees, particularly when it comes to employment matters. Historically, franchisees have been viewed as independent operators responsible for their own employees, but recent shifts in legal thinking have challenged this framework.

The **National Labor Relations Board (NLRB)** in the U.S. has been at the center of this debate, issuing rulings that in some cases broaden the definition of a joint employer. If a franchisor exerts significant control over a franchisee's employment practices, they may be deemed a joint employer, making them liable for labor law violations such as wage disputes, discrimination, or wrongful termination.

The potential implications of joint employer liability are profound:

• **Increased legal exposure:** Franchisors could face lawsuits and penalties related to their franchisees' employment practices.

• **Changes to operational control:** To minimize liability, some franchisors may reduce their control over franchisee operations, impacting the consistency of brand standards and service quality.

The ongoing legal and regulatory discussions about joint employer status highlight the importance of careful franchise agreement drafting to define the scope of control franchisors exert over franchisees.

2. Minimum Wage and Employment Law Changes

The push for a higher minimum wage and new employment laws has created challenges for franchisors and franchisees alike. In many jurisdictions, legislatures have raised minimum wage levels or enacted stricter labor regulations, which can significantly increase operational costs for franchisees. These changes often lead to tensions in the franchise relationship, particularly when franchisees are locked into fixed royalty and fee structures that do not account for rising labor costs.

Some franchisors have responded by allowing more operational flexibility, such as:

• **Adjusting fee structures:** Offering temporary reductions in royalty payments or other fees to help franchisees manage increased labor costs.

• **Introducing automation:** Encouraging the use of technology, such as automated kiosks or mobile ordering systems, to reduce labor reliance and help franchisees manage expenses.

Franchisors and franchisees must stay informed about changes in employment law, as non-compliance can result in costly litigation, penalties, and reputational damage.

3. DATA PRIVACY AND CYBERSECURITY LEGISLATION

As digital platforms and data-driven marketing become more integral to franchise operations, **data privacy** and **cybersecurity** regulations have taken on greater importance. Laws like the **General Data Protection Regulation (GDPR)** in Europe and the **California Consumer Privacy Act (CCPA)** in the United States have introduced stringent requirements for businesses that collect, store, and process personal data.

These regulations impact franchisors and franchisees in several ways:

• **Data security obligations:** Franchisees may be required to implement stronger security measures to protect customer data, such as encryption, secure payment processing systems, and regular security audits.

• **Customer consent:** Franchise systems that collect personal data for marketing purposes must ensure that customers give explicit consent and have the ability to access or delete their information.

• **Data breach liability:** In the event of a data breach, both franchisors and franchisees may face legal liability, especially if they fail to meet regulatory requirements for data protection.

As more jurisdictions introduce data privacy laws, franchisors must develop clear guidelines and provide ongoing support to help franchisees stay compliant.

EMERGING TRENDS IN FRANCHISE LITIGATION AND REGULATION

Franchising has always been a fertile ground for litigation, but recent years have seen a rise in disputes that reflect broader shifts in the legal and regulatory environment. Franchisees and franchisors are increasingly clashing over issues such as profitability, operational control, and the fairness of contractual terms.

. . .

1. Franchisee Profitability and Fair Dealings

One of the most contentious issues in franchise litigation is the question of franchisee profitability. Many franchisees have filed lawsuits claiming that franchisors failed to provide sufficient support or made misleading profitability claims in their Franchise Disclosure Documents (FDDs). These lawsuits often allege that the franchisor overstated revenue projections or downplayed the operational costs associated with running a franchise.

Several legal concepts are at play in these cases:

• **Good faith and fair dealing**: Many franchise agreements include a clause requiring both parties to act in good faith and engage in fair dealings. Franchisees may claim that franchisors violated this clause by failing to support their business or misrepresenting potential earnings.

• **Fraudulent misrepresentation**: If franchisees can prove that a franchisor knowingly provided false information during the franchise sales process, they may have grounds for a lawsuit based on fraudulent misrepresentation.

These cases highlight the importance of transparency in franchising, with franchisors needing to provide accurate, well-supported financial information in their FDDs.

2. Termination and Non-Renewal Disputes

Disputes over **termination** and **non-renewal** of franchise agreements have also become more frequent. Franchisees may claim that their agreements were terminated unfairly or without sufficient cause, while franchisors often argue that the franchisee violated the terms of the agreement, such as failing to meet performance standards or breaching operational guidelines.

In many jurisdictions, franchisors are required to provide notice of termination and give franchisees an opportunity to cure any deficiencies before the agreement can be terminated. However, disagreements over the sufficiency of notice, the severity of the breach, and the fairness of termination have led to numerous lawsuits.

3. ENCROACHMENT AND TERRITORIAL RIGHTS

As franchisors expand their brands, franchisees are increasingly concerned about **encroachment**, where new franchises or corporate-owned locations are opened too close to existing franchisee territories. This can dilute the market and reduce profitability for franchisees, leading to legal disputes over territorial rights.

Franchisees may argue that their exclusive territory rights are being violated, while franchisors contend that expansion is necessary for brand growth. These disputes often revolve around the wording of territorial clauses in franchise agreements and whether the franchisor is acting in good faith.

THE RISE OF FRANCHISEE ASSOCIATIONS AND COLLECTIVE BARGAINING

In response to these legal challenges, franchisees are increasingly banding together to form **franchisee associations** and engage in **collective bargaining**. These organizations give franchisees a collective voice, enabling them to negotiate more effectively with franchisors and advocate for their interests.

1. THE ROLE OF FRANCHISEE ASSOCIATIONS

Franchisee associations are independent organizations formed by franchisees within a specific franchise system. Their primary goal is to represent the collective interests of franchisees and advocate for fair treatment from franchisors. These associations can:

• **Negotiate on behalf of franchisees:** Associations can engage in collective bargaining with franchisors to negotiate better terms for all franchisees, such as reduced fees, more favorable contract terms, or additional support.

• **Provide legal support:** Franchisee associations often pool resources to hire legal counsel, allowing them to challenge unfair practices or take collective action against franchisors.

• **Share best practices:** Franchisees can benefit from the collective knowledge of their peers, sharing insights into operational efficiency, marketing strategies, and dispute resolution.

Many franchise systems have seen the rise of strong franchisee associations that have successfully negotiated better terms and conditions for their members.

2. Collective Bargaining in Franchising

While collective bargaining is more commonly associated with labor unions, it is gaining traction in the franchise industry as a way for franchisees to leverage their collective power. In recent years, franchisee associations have engaged in collective bargaining to address concerns such as:

• **Royalty and fee structures:** Franchisees may seek to renegotiate royalty rates, technology fees, or advertising contributions to reflect current market conditions and profitability.

• **Operational support:** Franchisees may collectively demand more robust training, marketing, or technology support from the franchisor.

• **Territorial protection:** Franchisee associations may advocate for stronger territorial protections to prevent encroachment and protect franchisees' market share.

Collective bargaining in franchising is still a relatively new trend, but it is gaining momentum as franchisees recognize the power of working together to achieve common goals.

3. Legal Considerations for Franchisee Associations

While franchisee associations can be powerful tools for advocating franchisee rights, they must operate within certain legal constraints. For example:

• **Antitrust concerns:** Franchisee associations must be careful not to engage in behavior that could be construed as collusion or price-fixing, which would violate antitrust laws.

- **Franchisor relations:** Franchisors may resist collective bargaining efforts, and franchise agreements may include clauses that limit franchisees' ability to form associations or engage in collective action.

Despite these challenges, the rise of franchisee associations signals a growing shift in the balance of power within franchise relationships.

Conclusion

The franchise industry is undergoing significant legal shifts, driven by changes in legislation, emerging litigation trends, and the rise of collective franchisee action. From joint employer liability and employment law changes to disputes over profitability and territorial rights, franchisors and franchisees must navigate an increasingly complex legal landscape. At the same time, the growth of franchisee associations and collective bargaining reflects a broader movement toward franchisees asserting greater control over their relationships with franchisors.

In this evolving environment, both franchisors and franchisees must remain informed, adaptable, and proactive in addressing the legal challenges that come with franchising in today's world. By staying ahead of legal trends and working collaboratively, franchisors and franchisees can build stronger, more sustainable partnerships for the future.

EPILOGUE

Franchising offers a unique and powerful path to business ownership, combining the independence of entrepreneurship with the support and structure of an established brand. However, as we have explored throughout this book, the journey of a franchisee is far more complex than simply signing an agreement and opening the doors to your location. It requires strategic planning, operational excellence, strong leadership, and the ability to navigate challenges and opportunities with vision and persistence.

From the initial decision to invest in a franchise to managing day-to-day operations, resolving disputes, and ultimately scaling your business, each phase of the franchise lifecycle demands attention to detail, a commitment to growth, and a passion for the brand you represent. Franchisees who thrive in this environment are those who embrace not only the opportunities that come with operating under a proven business model but also the responsibilities of upholding the brand's reputation and contributing to the long-term success of the franchise system as a whole.

KEY LESSONS FROM THE FRANCHISE JOURNEY

As we conclude, it's valuable to reflect on the **key lessons** covered in this book, each of which contributes to your ability to build and sustain a successful franchise business:

1. Choosing the Right Franchise Is Crucial

The foundation of any successful franchise journey begins with choosing the right franchise. This decision should be based on a careful assessment of your personal interests, skills, financial capacity, and long-term goals. The due diligence you conduct before signing the franchise agreement will help you identify a brand that aligns with your values and offers a sustainable business model in a market with growth potential.

2. Mastering Operations Leads to Consistency and Growth

Operational excellence is the cornerstone of any franchise business. As a franchisee, you must ensure that your location adheres to the franchisor's standards while continuously seeking ways to improve efficiency and customer satisfaction. A successful franchise operation is one that consistently delivers on the brand promise, which in turn fosters customer loyalty and supports long-term growth.

3. Strong Leadership Drives Success

Your role as a franchise leader is more than managing employees; it's about fostering a culture of success, motivating your team, and building future leaders. Effective leadership ensures that your business operates at peak performance and that your employees are engaged and empowered. Leadership also extends to strategic thinking, making key decisions, and ensuring that your business adapts to changing conditions while staying true to the franchisor's vision.

. . .

4. Scaling Requires Strategic Planning

If your goal is to grow beyond a single location, you must approach scaling with a **strategic plan.** Multi-unit franchise ownership offers the potential for significant financial rewards, but it also requires a strong operational foundation, effective delegation, and a focus on building an infrastructure that supports expansion. Scaling too quickly without proper systems in place can lead to operational inefficiencies, financial strain, and challenges in maintaining quality across all locations.

5. Disputes Are Inevitable, but Managing Them Well Is Key

Even the most well-run franchise businesses may face disputes, whether they arise from financial disagreements, territorial issues, or non-compliance with the franchise agreement. Knowing how to manage these disputes, whether through negotiation, mediation, or arbitration, is critical to protecting your business and maintaining a positive relationship with your franchisor.

6. Long-Term Success Comes from Adaptability and Innovation

The most successful franchisees are those who embrace change, stay informed about industry trends, and continually innovate. As markets shift and customer preferences evolve, franchisees must be ready to adapt their strategies, embrace new technologies, and find creative ways to meet changing demands. Remaining adaptable and forward-thinking ensures that your franchise stays competitive and positioned for long-term success.

Building a Lasting Legacy in Franchising

For many franchisees, the ultimate goal is to build a business that creates **lasting value**—whether that means passing the franchise on to future generations, selling the business for a substantial return, or continuing to expand into new territories. Building a lasting legacy in franchising is about more than financial success; it's about creating something sustainable that contributes to the community, provides opportunities for employees, and strengthens the franchise brand.

To build a legacy, franchisees must invest in both their business and their personal development. This means continually improving leadership skills, mentoring future leaders, staying engaged with the franchise system, and finding ways to give back to the community. Franchisees who focus on long-term success, rather than short-term gains, are those who leave a positive mark on their business, their employees, and the industry as a whole.

Looking Ahead: Your Franchise Journey

The world of franchising offers limitless opportunities for those willing to embrace its challenges and rewards. Whether you are just starting your franchise journey or are an experienced multi-unit owner looking to take your business to the next level, the lessons outlined in this book provide a roadmap for success. By approaching each stage of the franchise lifecycle with careful planning, a commitment to excellence, and a focus on leadership, you can build a thriving franchise business that stands the test of time.

The franchise journey is not without its ups and downs, but with the right mindset, strategy, and support, you can navigate its complexities and achieve lasting success. Now, it's up to you to take the insights from this book and apply them to your own franchise, turning your vision into reality and building a business that thrives in the years to come.

Your franchise journey begins now. The future is bright, and the opportunities are endless. Embrace the challenges, lead with confidence, and build the business of your dreams.

Here's to your success in franchising!

RESOURCES

FRANCHISE DISCLOSURE DOCUMENT (FDD) CHECKLIST:
A GUIDE FOR REVIEWING KEY SECTIONS

When reviewing a Franchise Disclosure Document (FDD), prospective franchisees should pay close attention to several critical sections to ensure they fully understand the franchise opportunity, the associated obligations, and the risks involved. Here's a checklist to guide you through the most important sections:

1. FRANCHISOR AND ANY PARENTS, PREDECESSORS, AND AFFILIATES (Item 1)

• **What to look for:** Overview of the franchisor, its history, corporate structure, and any related entities.

• **Questions to ask:**

◦ How long has the franchisor been in operation?

◦ Are there any significant corporate changes that could impact your franchise?

2. BUSINESS EXPERIENCE (ITEM 2)

- **What to look for:** The professional background of key executives in the franchisor's organization.
  - **Questions to ask:**
  - ○ Does the management team have experience in franchising or the industry?
  - ○ Is their experience relevant to supporting your success?

3. Litigation History (Item 3)

- **What to look for:** Any past or pending litigation involving the franchisor, its officers, or other franchisees.
  - **Questions to ask:**
  - ○ Are there significant legal disputes that could indicate problems within the franchise system?
  - ○ Are there any patterns of franchisee-franchisor conflicts?

4. Bankruptcy (Item 4)

- **What to look for:** Information on any bankruptcy filings involving the franchisor or its principals.
  - **Questions to ask:**
  - ○ Has the franchisor been involved in any recent bankruptcies?
  - ○ What was the outcome of any financial difficulties?

5. Initial Fees (Item 5)

- **What to look for:** A breakdown of the initial franchise fees you are required to pay.
  - **Questions to ask:**
  - ○ Are the fees reasonable compared to similar franchises?
  - ○ What do the fees cover (e.g., training, opening support)?

6. Other Fees (Item 6)

• **What to look for:** Ongoing fees such as royalties, marketing fees, technology fees, etc.
  • **Questions to ask:**
  ◦ Are there caps or limits on fees?
  ◦ How do the fees compare with other franchise opportunities?

7. INITIAL INVESTMENT (ITEM 7)

• **What to look for:** A detailed estimate of the initial investment required, including startup costs, equipment, and inventory.
  • **Questions to ask:**
  ◦ Are the projections realistic for your market?
  ◦ Do you have the financial capacity to cover unexpected expenses?

8. RESTRICTIONS ON SOURCES OF PRODUCTS AND SERVICES (ITEM 8)

• **What to look for:** Information about required suppliers and restrictions on where you can source products.
  • **Questions to ask:**
  ◦ Are there exclusive suppliers, and if so, are their prices competitive?
  ◦ Can you negotiate better terms if sourcing from other vendors?

9. FRANCHISEE'S OBLIGATIONS (ITEM 9)

• **What to look for:** A list of your obligations under the franchise agreement, including operational, financial, and advertising responsibilities.
  • **Questions to ask:**
  ◦ Are the obligations reasonable and feasible for your situation?
  ◦ What happens if you fail to meet these obligations?

· · ·

10. FINANCING (ITEM 10)

• **What to look for:** Information on financing assistance or options provided by the franchisor.

• **Questions to ask:**

◦ Does the franchisor offer financing or have relationships with preferred lenders?

◦ Are the terms competitive and favorable?

11. FRANCHISOR'S ASSISTANCE, ADVERTISING, COMPUTER SYSTEMS, AND Training (Item 11)

• **What to look for:** Details of the support you will receive from the franchisor.

• **Questions to ask:**

◦ What training is offered, and how comprehensive is it?

◦ Is there ongoing support, especially regarding marketing and technology?

12. TERRITORY (ITEM 12)

• **What to look for:** Information on the territory you will operate in and whether it is exclusive.

• **Questions to ask:**

◦ Is the territory large enough to support your business?

◦ Are there any conditions under which the franchisor could reduce your territory?

13. TRADEMARKS (ITEM 13)

• **What to look for:** Information about the trademarks you will be using as a franchisee.

• **Questions to ask:**

◦ Are the trademarks protected, and is the franchisor actively enforcing their rights?

◦ Could there be any legal disputes over the use of trademarks in your territory?

14. PATENTS, COPYRIGHTS, AND PROPRIETARY INFORMATION (ITEM 14)
- **What to look for:** Details on any intellectual property that you will have access to as a franchisee.
- **Questions to ask:**
◦ Are there key technologies or systems that give this franchise a competitive advantage?
◦ Are you protected if there is a legal challenge?

15. OBLIGATION TO PARTICIPATE IN THE ACTUAL OPERATION OF THE Franchise Business (Item 15)
- **What to look for:** Whether you are required to personally operate the franchise or hire an approved manager.
- **Questions to ask:**
◦ Can you hire a manager, or are you required to be an owner-operator?
◦ What qualifications are required for key personnel?

16. RESTRICTIONS ON WHAT THE FRANCHISEE MAY SELL (ITEM 16)
- **What to look for:** Any limitations on the products or services you can offer.
- **Questions to ask:**
◦ Are the restrictions reasonable and flexible to allow you to meet market demands?
◦ Can you add products or services to boost revenue?

17. RENEWAL, TERMINATION, TRANSFER, AND DISPUTE RESOLUTION (Item 17)

• **What to look for:** Information about your rights and obligations regarding renewing or terminating the franchise, selling it, and handling disputes.

   • **Questions to ask:**

   ◦ Are the renewal terms favorable?

   ◦ What are the termination conditions, and are they fair to you?

   ◦ How are disputes handled—through arbitration, litigation, or mediation?

18. PUBLIC FIGURES (ITEM 18)

• **What to look for:** Any celebrities or public figures associated with the franchise.

   • **Questions to ask:**

   ◦ How does the involvement of public figures impact the brand's reputation?

   ◦ Are you paying extra for their involvement?

19. FINANCIAL PERFORMANCE REPRESENTATIONS (ITEM 19)

• **What to look for:** Any earnings claims or financial projections provided by the franchisor.

   • **Questions to ask:**

   ◦ Are the numbers backed by solid data, and how do they compare with your research?

   ◦ How much does your specific location impact your potential earnings?

20. OUTLETS AND FRANCHISEE INFORMATION (ITEM 20)

• **What to look for:** Data on the number of franchises, terminations, transfers, and non-renewals.

   • **Questions to ask:**

   ◦ Are there significant numbers of closures or terminations that could be a red flag?

◦ What is the growth trend for the franchise system?

21. FINANCIAL STATEMENTS (ITEM 21)
- **What to look for:** The franchisor's audited financial statements.
- **Questions to ask:**
◦ Does the franchisor appear financially stable?
◦ Are there any red flags indicating financial instability?

22. CONTRACTS (ITEM 22)
- **What to look for:** Copies of all agreements you will need to sign as a franchisee, including the franchise agreement and any leases.
- **Questions to ask:**
◦ Are the terms reasonable, and do they align with the disclosures made in the FDD?
◦ Do you need a lawyer to review the contract before signing?

23. RECEIPTS (ITEM 23)
- **What to look for:** Acknowledgement of receipt of the FDD.
- **Questions to ask:**
◦ Have you kept a copy of your signed receipt, and was the FDD provided to you within the legal timeframe?

ADDITIONAL TIPS:
- **Consult with an attorney:** Franchising is a significant legal commitment. It's essential to have a franchise attorney review the FDD and provide advice on the legal implications.
- **Speak with current franchisees:** Ask about their experiences, profitability, and any unexpected challenges.
- **Do your research:** Compare this franchise opportunity with others in the same industry to assess its value and potential for success.

. . .

THIS CHECKLIST SERVES AS A GUIDE, BUT ALWAYS SEEK PROFESSIONAL advice before making any final decisions regarding a franchise investment.

10 ITEMS TO ASK OTHER FRANCHISEES

INSIGHTFUL QUESTIONS THAT POTENTIAL FRANCHISEES SHOULD ASK EXISTING FRANCHISE OWNERS, ALONG WITH COMMENTARY ON WHY EACH QUESTION IS IMPORTANT:

1. **How long did it take you to break even?**
   - **Why Ask:** Understanding the timeline for reaching profitability gives insight into the financial demands of the business and how long it may take to recover the initial investment.

2. **ARE YOU SATISFIED WITH THE SUPPORT FROM THE FRANCHISOR?**
   - **Why Ask:** A franchisee's experience with franchisor support—such as marketing, training, and operational assistance—is key to determining how well the franchisor equips its franchisees for success.

3. **WHAT ARE THE BIGGEST CHALLENGES YOU'VE FACED?**
   - **Why Ask:** Knowing the common obstacles helps a potential franchisee prepare and assess if they are ready to handle similar issues.

4. **WHAT DO YOU WISH YOU KNEW BEFORE JOINING THE FRANCHISE?**

• **Why Ask:** Hearing about "unknown unknowns" can reveal potential pitfalls or areas of concern that might not be obvious from just reading the franchise disclosure document (FDD) or speaking with the franchisor.

5. How would you rate the marketing support and materials provided by the franchisor?

• **Why Ask:** Strong marketing support is crucial for driving customer traffic, especially in the early stages of business. It's important to learn if the marketing promises align with actual experiences.

6. How often are the royalty fees or other expenses increased?

• **Why Ask:** Fees can eat into profit margins over time, and it's important to understand the franchisor's history and policies on fee increases.

7. How do you manage the balance between franchisor rules and local market conditions?

• **Why Ask:** Every market is different, and some franchise models may be more flexible than others in allowing franchisees to adapt to their local market conditions. This question highlights the franchisor's flexibility and openness to local modifications.

8. Is there a strong sense of community and collaboration among franchisees?

• **Why Ask:** A supportive network of fellow franchisees can provide valuable advice and camaraderie. Knowing how franchisees interact and support one another is important for fostering a collaborative environment.

. . .

9. Have you encountered any legal or contractual issues?

• **Why Ask:** Learning about past disputes or concerns related to the franchise agreement or operational guidelines can shed light on potential risks.

10. Would you do it again if you had the choice?

• **Why Ask:** This is a powerful, straightforward question that speaks volumes about the overall franchisee experience. If the owner would repeat their investment, it's generally a good sign.

These questions help provide an in-depth view of the franchise system, beyond what's presented in the formal documents, giving a potential franchisee a clearer picture of what to expect.

BASIC GUIDE FOR NEGOTIATING A COMMERCIAL LEASE

TIPS FOR NEGOTIATING YOUR FIRST LOCATION WITH A LANDLORD

Negotiating a commercial lease is a critical step for any franchisee. The terms of the lease can have a significant impact on the profitability and long-term success of your franchise. Here's a guide with key tips for negotiating a fair lease and common provisions that may require careful consideration or negotiation.

Tips for Negotiating a Fair Lease

1 Understand Market Rates

Research the local market to ensure the rent and terms you are being offered align with comparable properties in the area. If the lease terms seem above market, use this data to negotiate.

2 Request Tenant Improvement (TI) Allowances

Many landlords offer TI allowances to help cover renovation or build-out costs. Negotiate for as much TI funding as possible, particularly if significant modifications are needed to meet franchise requirements.

3 Negotiate Rent Increases

Avoid steep rent escalations by negotiating a cap on annual increases, either at a fixed percentage or tied to the Consumer Price Index (CPI). Ideally, secure fixed-rate increases to avoid unpredictable costs.

4 Lease Term and Renewal Options

Secure a lease term that aligns with your franchise agreement, and negotiate multiple renewal options at pre-agreed terms. Shorter terms with renewal options offer flexibility in case your business needs change.

5 Negotiate Free Rent Periods

Try to negotiate a rent abatement or free rent period at the start of the lease. This can provide relief as you prepare and open the business, giving you time to generate revenue before paying full rent.

6 Examine and Limit Personal Guaranties

Be cautious of personal guarantees. If required, negotiate to limit their scope or the time period during which they apply. Also, consider negotiating for a "burn-off" clause where personal liability decreases over time as the business becomes more established.

7 Consider Subleasing or Assignment Rights

Negotiate the right to sublease or assign the lease if you decide to sell your franchise. This flexibility can be critical if you want to exit the business early or transfer the franchise.

8 WATCH FOR HIDDEN COSTS

Clarify any hidden costs that may be included in the lease, such as common area maintenance (CAM) fees, property taxes, or utilities. Try to negotiate caps or limits on these expenses.

9 SEEK LEGAL AND PROFESSIONAL ADVICE

Have an attorney and a commercial real estate professional review the lease before signing. Their expertise will help identify any unfavorable terms and ensure you're getting a fair deal.

COMMONLY INCLUDED LEASE PROVISIONS THAT MAY REQUIRE Negotiation

1 RENT AND RENT ESCALATION

The rent structure, including base rent and any percentage rent, should be clear and predictable. Ensure that rent escalation clauses are reasonable and not tied to arbitrary benchmarks.

2 COMMON AREA MAINTENANCE (CAM) CHARGES

CAM charges are often negotiable. Request a detailed breakdown of these costs and try to negotiate a cap on annual increases or limit what types of expenses are included.

3 EXCLUSIVE USE CLAUSES

Ensure you negotiate for an exclusive use clause that prevents the landlord from leasing to direct competitors in the same building or complex. This helps protect your market share and customer base.

4 Maintenance and Repair Responsibilities

Clarify which party is responsible for maintenance and repairs. Franchisees should seek to limit their responsibility for structural repairs or significant maintenance items.

5 Signage and Visibility

Negotiate signage rights to ensure your franchise is visible and can attract customers. Confirm that any signage complies with franchise brand standards, and negotiate for favorable placement within the property.

6 Permitted Use

Review the permitted use clause carefully. Ensure that it allows for any future franchise model adjustments or expansions that may be introduced by the franchisor during your lease term.

7 Operating Hours and Co-tenancy Clauses

If the lease requires specific operating hours, make sure they align with the franchise's standard business model. Additionally, negotiate a co-tenancy clause that allows you to renegotiate rent or terminate the lease if key anchor tenants vacate the property.

8 Option to Renew or Extend

Negotiate favorable renewal options. Ensure the lease includes pre-set terms for renewal so you can secure your location without large rent hikes when the original lease expires.

. . .

9 Termination Clauses

Review any early termination or default clauses carefully. Try to negotiate flexible terms that allow you to exit or reduce your liabilities if the franchise faces challenges or the location becomes undesirable.

10 Force Majeure Clauses

In light of unforeseen events (such as natural disasters or pandemics), ensure the lease includes a force majeure clause that allows for rent relief or a temporary pause in obligations in cases of events beyond your control.

———

Final Thoughts

Negotiating a commercial lease as a franchisee is a crucial process that requires a clear understanding of your rights, potential obligations, and the flexibility needed to ensure your franchise can thrive. By carefully reviewing each provision and negotiating terms that protect your interests, you can set your business up for long-term success. Always seek expert advice and take the time to understand the full scope of your lease agreement before signing.

EXIT STRATEGY AND SUCCESSION PLANNING CHECKLIST FOR FRANCHISEES

Planning your exit from a franchise or preparing for succession requires careful consideration and strategic steps. This checklist is designed to guide franchisees through the key elements involved in both exiting the business and ensuring a smooth transition of ownership.

I. REVIEW FRANCHISE AGREEMENT FOR EXIT PROVISIONS

- **UNDERSTAND TRANSFER RESTRICTIONS:**
  - Review the franchise agreement to identify any restrictions on selling, transferring, or exiting the business.
  - Look for clauses regarding franchisor approval for transfers.
  - **Determine Required Fees:**
  - Check for any transfer fees, exit fees, or administrative charges imposed by the franchisor for selling or transferring the franchise.
  - **Understand Non-Compete Clauses:**
  - Review non-compete clauses that may limit your ability to engage in similar businesses after exit.

---

2. Determine the Value of Your Franchise
- **Hire a Business Valuator:**
  ◦ Engage a professional to assess the market value of the franchise.
  ◦ Consider earnings, assets, brand value, and local market conditions.
- **Review Financial Statements:**
  ◦ Prepare recent financial statements (profit and loss, balance sheet, etc.) to provide to potential buyers.
- **Calculate Intangible Value:**
  ◦ Factor in goodwill, customer base, and other intangible assets that add value to the business.

---

3. Prepare the Franchise for Sale or Transfer
- **Ensure Compliance with Franchisor Requirements:**
  ◦ Make sure the franchise is fully compliant with franchisor standards, including operational guidelines, marketing materials, and branding.
- **Update Legal and Financial Documents:**
  ◦ Ensure all legal and financial documents are up to date, including tax filings, employee agreements, and lease agreements.
- **Clean Up Operations:**
  ◦ Streamline operations to make the business more attractive to buyers (e.g., modernize processes, improve customer relations, and reduce inefficiencies).

---

4. Find a Suitable Buyer
- **Identify Potential Buyers:**

- ○ Work with a business broker, or advertise through franchise resale platforms to find potential buyers.
- ○ Consider selling to family members, current employees, or another franchisee within the system.
- **Franchisor's Right of First Refusal:**
- ○ Check if the franchisor has the right of first refusal, meaning they can choose to buy your franchise before you sell to an external party.
- **Vet Buyers:**
- ○ Ensure the buyer meets the financial and operational qualifications required by the franchisor.

———

5. **FRANCHISOR APPROVAL PROCESS**
- **Submit Transfer Application:**
- ○ Prepare a formal transfer application and submit it to the franchisor for approval.
- **Provide Buyer's Qualifications:**
- ○ Present the buyer's qualifications, including financial standing, experience, and business plans.
- **Complete Franchisor's Transfer Training:**
- ○ Ensure the buyer completes any necessary training programs mandated by the franchisor before the transfer is finalized.

———

6. **LEGAL AND FINANCIAL CONSIDERATIONS FOR TRANSFER**
- **Transfer of Lease or Property:**
- ○ Review the lease to determine if it can be assigned to the buyer or if the landlord's consent is needed for the transfer.
- **Tax Implications:**
- ○ Consult with an accountant or tax advisor to understand the tax consequences of selling the franchise, including capital gains taxes and other liabilities.

• **Draft a Purchase Agreement:**

◦ Work with an attorney to draft a comprehensive purchase agreement outlining the terms and conditions of the sale.

––––––

7. **EMPLOYEE AND CUSTOMER TRANSITION**

• **Communicate with Employees:**

◦ Inform key employees about the potential transition and discuss employment terms with the new owner.

◦ Ensure continuity in management to ease the transition for employees.

• **Customer Relations:**

◦ Plan to inform loyal customers about the transition in a way that ensures continued patronage.

◦ Coordinate with the new owner to maintain customer satisfaction and brand loyalty during the transition.

––––––

8. **PLAN FOR PERSONAL TRANSITION AND NON-COMPETE COMPLIANCE**

• **Comply with Non-Compete Clauses:**

◦ Review the non-compete obligations in the franchise agreement and plan accordingly if you intend to pursue new ventures.

• **Personal Financial Planning:**

◦ Plan your personal financial future after the sale, including the management of proceeds and future investments.

• **Prepare for Post-Exit Role:**

◦ Consider whether you want to remain involved as a consultant or transition out of the industry entirely.

––––––

9. **SUCCESSION PLANNING FOR FAMILY OR INTERNAL TRANSFER**

• **Develop a Succession Plan:**

◦ If transferring to a family member or key employee, create a formal succession plan to ensure a smooth transition of ownership.

• **Prepare Successor for Franchisor Approval:**

◦ Ensure the successor meets the franchisor's qualifications and training requirements.

• **Legal and Estate Planning:**

◦ Work with an attorney to ensure the transfer aligns with your estate planning and that ownership is properly documented.

―――

10. FINALIZE THE TRANSITION

• **Close Financial Accounts:**

◦ Transition bank accounts, credit lines, and other financial agreements to the new owner.

• **Handover Operations and Training:**

◦ Provide support and guidance during the handover period to ensure the new owner is well-prepared.

• **Notify Key Stakeholders:**

◦ Inform key suppliers, service providers, and customers of the ownership change.

―――

RESOURCES FOR FRANCHISE EXIT AND SUCCESSION PLANNING:

• **Business Valuation Services:** Contact a professional franchise business appraiser.

• **Franchise Resale Platforms:** Explore platforms like Franchise-Flippers, BizBuySell, or Franchise Resales to list your business.

• **Legal and Tax Advisors:** Work with attorneys and tax professionals to manage the financial and legal aspects of your exit.

• **Franchisor's Transfer Guidelines:** Obtain specific guidelines from the franchisor regarding the sale or transfer process.

• **Estate Planning Resources:** Ensure succession aligns with broader estate planning goals through proper legal documentation.

———

Final Thoughts

Creating an exit strategy or succession plan is essential to protect your investment and ensure the franchise's continued success after your departure. By following this checklist, you can help ensure that the process is smooth, legally sound, and financially beneficial for all parties involved. Always seek professional advice from legal, financial, and tax advisors to navigate the complexities of the process.

GLOSSARY OF FRANCHISE TERMS

A COMPREHENSIVE LIST OF LEGAL AND INDUSTRY-SPECIFIC TERMS COMMONLY USED IN FRANCHISE LAW AND AGREEMENTS

Area Developer

- A franchisee who has the right and obligation to open multiple franchise units in a specified area within a certain timeframe.

Assignment

- The ability of the franchisee to transfer their rights under the franchise agreement to another party, typically subject to the franchisor's approval.

Audit Rights

- The franchisor's right to inspect the franchisee's financial records to ensure compliance with the agreement, particularly regarding the calculation of royalty fees.

Brand Standards

- The guidelines and specifications that franchisees must follow to maintain consistency and uniformity in the brand's products, services, and appearance.

Confidentiality Agreement

◦ A clause in the franchise agreement requiring the franchisee to keep certain proprietary information confidential, such as trade secrets, business methods, or operational procedures.

Continuing Franchise Fee

◦ A recurring fee paid by the franchisee to the franchisor, which can be a fixed amount or a percentage of gross sales (often the same as or included in royalty fees).

Continuity of Operations

◦ The franchisor's and franchisee's plans for maintaining business operations during disruptions, such as natural disasters or other crises.

Conversion Franchise

◦ A franchise where an existing independent business is converted into a franchise unit under the franchisor's brand.

Cure Period

◦ A specified time during which a defaulting party (usually the franchisee) has the opportunity to correct a breach before the franchisor can terminate the agreement.

De-identification

• The process by which a franchisee removes all branding and intellectual property from the business following the termination of the franchise agreement.

DEFAULT

- A breach of the franchise agreement by either party, typically involving failure to comply with specified obligations, such as paying fees or adhering to operational standards.

DEFAULT NOTICE

- A formal notification from the franchisor to the franchisee that they have breached the franchise agreement, often triggering a cure period.

DEVELOPMENT AGREEMENT

- A contract between the franchisor and franchisee (or area developer) outlining the rights and obligations related to opening multiple units within a certain area.

DEVELOPMENT SCHEDULE

- A timeline included in the franchise agreement or development agreement outlining when and where new franchise units must be opened by the franchisee.

DISCLOSURE OBLIGATIONS

- The franchisor's legal requirement to provide specific information (e.g., the FDD) to prospective franchisees before the sale of a franchise.

DISPUTE RESOLUTION CLAUSE

• A section of the franchise agreement that outlines the methods for resolving disputes between the franchisor and franchisee, such as mediation or arbitration.

Earned Royalties

• Royalties that have accrued based on the franchisee's sales and must be paid to the franchisor, regardless of the franchisee's profitability.

Encroachment

• When a franchisor allows another franchise location or corporate-owned store to operate within or near an existing franchisee's territory, potentially affecting the franchisee's business.

Encumbrances

• Restrictions or claims on the property or assets of the franchisee, such as liens or mortgages, that could affect the franchise operation.

Encumbrances on Franchise Business

• Legal claims or liens placed on the franchisee's assets or franchise unit, which could affect the franchisee's ability to operate or sell the business.

Exclusive Territory

• A designated area where no other franchisees or franchisor-owned locations are allowed to operate.

Failure to Cure

• When a franchisee does not correct a breach of the franchise agreement within the given cure period, leading to possible termination.

Financial Performance Representations (FPR)

• A statement in the FDD that provides prospective franchisees with data on the financial performance of existing franchise locations, if the franchisor chooses to include it.

Force Majeure

• A clause that excuses the franchisor or franchisee from liability or performance obligations due to events beyond their control, such as natural disasters or pandemics.

Franchise Advisory Board

• A formal body composed of franchisees who provide input and recommendations to the franchisor on system-wide policies and practices.

Franchise Agreement

• The legal contract between the franchisor and the franchisee that sets out the rights and obligations of each party.

Franchise Broker

• A third party who helps match prospective franchisees with franchise opportunities, often earning a commission from the franchisor.

Franchise Churning

• A practice where the franchisor frequently terminates or resells franchises to new franchisees, often to generate additional initial franchise fees.

FRANCHISE DISCLOSURE DOCUMENT (FDD)

• A legal document that franchisors must provide to prospective franchisees before signing an agreement. It contains key details about the franchise system, fees, litigation history, financial performance, and other critical aspects.

FRANCHISE FEE

• A one-time fee paid by the franchisee to the franchisor for the right to operate a franchise. This is separate from ongoing fees such as royalties.

FRANCHISE REGISTRY

• A database that lists franchises that have registered and complied with certain regulatory requirements, often used to help lenders and investors assess franchise opportunities.

FRANCHISE SYSTEM

• The comprehensive set of procedures, products, services, and support provided by the franchisor to franchisees, designed to create uniformity across all franchise units.

FRANCHISEE

• The individual or entity that purchases the right to operate a franchise business under the franchisor's brand and system.

. . .

Franchisee Advisory Council (FAC)

- A group of franchisees that provides feedback and advice to the franchisor on issues affecting the franchise system, often in an advisory role.

Franchisor

- The entity or person that owns the franchise system and grants the right to operate a franchise to franchisees.

Good Faith and Fair Dealing

- A legal principle that requires both the franchisor and franchisee to act honestly and fairly in their dealings with each other, often implied in the franchise agreement.

Good Standing Certificate

- A document that certifies the franchisee's compliance with state or local regulations and the terms of the franchise agreement.

Goodwill

- The established reputation of the franchise and brand that is considered an intangible asset, often part of the franchise value.

Grand Opening

- The initial marketing and promotional activities that occur when a new franchise location opens, often with specific guidelines and support from the franchisor.

Gross Sales

- The total revenue generated by the franchisee before any

deductions such as taxes, returns, or discounts, often used as a basis for calculating royalty fees.

In-Term Non-Compete

• A clause that restricts the franchisee from engaging in any business that competes with the franchisor's brand during the term of the franchise agreement.

Indemnification

• A contractual provision where one party agrees to compensate the other for certain losses or damages, often related to third-party claims.

Initial Franchise Fee

• The upfront fee paid by the franchisee to the franchisor for the right to enter into a franchise relationship and use the franchisor's brand and systems.

Initial Investment

• The total amount of money a franchisee is required to invest to start and operate the franchise, including franchise fees, real estate, equipment, and working capital.

Initial Training Program

• The first set of training provided by the franchisor to help the franchisee start and operate the franchise according to the franchisor's standards.

Intellectual Property (IP)

• The franchisor's trademarks, service marks, logos, and other proprietary information that the franchisee is licensed to use.

Liquidated Damages

• Pre-determined compensation outlined in the franchise agreement that a franchisee may owe the franchisor if the franchise agreement is terminated early under certain conditions.

Liquidated Damages Clause

• A clause in the agreement specifying the amount of compensation the franchisor is entitled to if the agreement is prematurely terminated by the franchisee.

Marketing/Advertising Fund Fee

• A fee franchisees pay into a collective fund used by the franchisor for system-wide marketing and advertising efforts.

Master Franchise

• A type of franchise agreement where the master franchisee has the right to sell and manage franchises within a certain region or country, often acting as a mini-franchisor.

Minimum Performance Requirements

• Benchmarks that franchisees must meet, such as minimum sales targets, operational standards, or customer satisfaction levels.

Multi-Unit Development Rights

• The rights granted to a franchisee to open and operate multiple franchise locations within a specific region.

. . .

Multi-Unit Franchise

• A franchise arrangement where the franchisee operates more than one franchise location, either simultaneously or over time.

Net Operating Income (NOI)

• A financial metric used to measure the profitability of a franchise location after deducting operating expenses but before taxes and interest.

Non-Compete Clause

• A restriction that prevents the franchisee from operating a competing business during and after the term of the franchise agreement, usually for a specified duration and geographic area.

Non-Disclosure Agreement (NDA)

• A legal agreement requiring the franchisee (or prospective franchisee) to keep proprietary information, such as trade secrets or financial data, confidential.

Non-Exclusive Territory

• A geographic area where the franchisee may operate but could potentially face competition from other franchisees or the franchisor itself.

Operating Manual

• A detailed set of instructions provided by the franchisor that outlines how the franchisee must operate the franchise to ensure consistency and compliance with the franchise system.

. . .

Operations Support

• Ongoing assistance provided by the franchisor to the franchisee, which can include training, technology updates, marketing advice, and more.

Performance Default

• A breach of the franchise agreement due to failure to meet specified operational standards, such as failing to meet sales targets or maintain quality control.

Personal Guarantee

• A legal commitment where an individual (often the franchisee) agrees to be personally liable for the debts and obligations of the franchise business.

Post-Term Non-Compete

• A restriction that prevents the franchisee from engaging in a competing business for a specified period and within a defined geographic area after the franchise agreement has ended.

Post-Termination Obligations

• The franchisee's responsibilities after the termination of the franchise agreement, such as ceasing the use of trademarks, returning proprietary materials, or de-branding.

Pre-Opening Expenses

• Costs incurred by the franchisee before the franchise business opens, such as real estate, training, equipment, and initial inventory.

. . .

Product Exclusivity

- A requirement that franchisees sell only franchisor-approved or provided products, preventing them from offering unauthorized goods or services.

Protected Marks

- Trademarks, service marks, and other branding elements that are legally protected and must be used correctly by the franchisee.

Protected Territory

- A geographic area where the franchisee has exclusive rights to operate and within which no other franchisee or company-owned store can compete.

Quality Control

- The process by which the franchisor monitors and ensures that the franchisee maintains the standards of the brand, including product quality and customer service.

Rebranding Costs

- Expenses incurred by the franchisee to update the franchise location's appearance, signage, or other branding elements in accordance with the franchisor's system-wide changes.

Renewal Terms

- Provisions that allow the franchisee to renew the franchise agreement for additional terms, usually under specified conditions.

. . .

Resale Rights

- The ability of the franchisee to sell their franchise unit to another party, subject to the franchisor's approval.

Resale Value

- The market value of an existing franchise unit when the franchisee decides to sell it to a new franchisee, often influenced by the unit's profitability and market conditions.

Rescission Rights

- The franchisee's right to cancel the franchise agreement under certain conditions, typically due to misrepresentation or failure of the franchisor to comply with disclosure requirements.

Royalty Fee

- An ongoing fee, typically a percentage of gross sales, that the franchisee must pay to the franchisor for continued use of the franchisor's brand, systems, and support.

Site Approval

- The franchisor's requirement that the franchisee obtains approval for the business location to ensure it meets the franchisor's criteria, such as market potential, traffic flow, and visibility.

Sub-Franchise

- A franchise that operates under the master franchisee, where the sub-franchisee pays fees to both the master franchisee and the original franchisor.

. . .

Sublease

• An arrangement where the franchisee leases premises from the franchisor rather than directly from the property owner, sometimes with additional rental fees or terms.

Supplier Rebates

• Payments made by suppliers to the franchisor based on franchisee purchases, which may or may not be disclosed to franchisees.

Supply Chain Control

• The franchisor's authority to dictate where franchisees must purchase products and supplies, often from approved or exclusive vendors.

Supply Chain/Approved Suppliers

• The network of vendors or suppliers approved by the franchisor for franchisees to use, ensuring consistency in product quality and availability.

System-wide Change

• A modification or update implemented by the franchisor that affects all franchisees in the system, such as menu changes, rebranding, or new technology implementation.

Technology Fee

• A fee paid by the franchisee to cover the cost of software, hardware, or technological support provided by the franchisor, often for point-of-sale systems or online ordering platforms.

.   .   .

TERMINATION CLAUSE
- A section of the franchise agreement that details the circumstances under which the agreement can be terminated by either party.

TERRITORY
- The geographic area in which the franchisee has the right to operate the franchise. This may be exclusive (no other franchisees in the area) or non-exclusive.

TRADE DRESS
- The distinctive appearance or design of the franchised business, which is protected under trademark law, and which franchisees must replicate to maintain brand consistency.

TRADEMARK INFRINGEMENT
- Unauthorized use of the franchisor's trademarks or logos by the franchisee or third parties, which could harm the brand's reputation.

TRAINING PROGRAMS
- Instruction provided by the franchisor to the franchisee on how to operate the franchise, including initial and ongoing training.

TRANSFER FEE
- A fee charged by the franchisor when a franchisee sells or transfers their franchise to another individual or entity, subject to franchisor approval.

FRANCHISE RULE - 16 CFR PART 436

presumption that the seller failed to comply with said requirement.

§ 435.3 Limited applicability.

(a) This part shall not apply to:

(1) Subscriptions, such as magazine sales, ordered for serial delivery, after the initial shipment is made in compliance with this part;

(2) Orders of seeds and growing plants;

(3) Orders made on a collect-on-delivery (C.O.D.) basis;

(4) Transactions governed by the Federal Trade Commission's Trade Regulation Rule entitled "Use of Prenotification Negative Option Plans," 16 CFR Part 425.

(b) By taking action in this area:

(1) The Federal Trade Commission does not intend to preempt action in the same area, which is not inconsistent with this part, by any State, municipal, or other local government. This part does not annul or diminish any rights or remedies provided to consumers by any State law, municipal ordinance, or other local regulation, insofar as those rights or remedies are equal to or greater than those provided by this part. In addition, this part does not supersede those provisions of any State law, municipal ordinance, or other local regulation which impose obligations or liabilities upon sellers, when sellers subject to this part are not in compliance therewith.

(2) This part does supersede those provisions of any State law, municipal ordinance, or other local regulation which are inconsistent with this part to the extent that those provisions do not provide a buyer with rights which are equal to or greater than those rights granted a buyer by this part. This part also supersedes those provisions of any State law, municipal ordinance, or other local regulation requiring that a buyer be notified of a right which is the same as a right provided by this part but requiring that a buyer be given notice of this right in a language, form, or manner which is different in any way from that required by this part. In those instances where any State law, municipal ordinance, or other local regulation contains provisions, some but not all of which are partially or completely superseded by

this part, the provisions or portions of those provisions which have not been superseded retain their full force and effect.

(c) If any provision of this part, or its application to any person, partnership, corporation, act or practice is held invalid, the remainder of this part or the application of the provision to any other person, partnership, corporation, act or practice shall not be affected thereby.

PART 436—DISCLOSURE REQUIREMENTS AND PROHIBITIONS CONCERNING FRANCHISING

Subpart A—Definitions

Sec.
436.1 Definitions.

Subpart B—Franchisor's Obligations

436.2 Obligation to furnish documents.

Subpart C—Contents of a Disclosure Document

436.3 Cover page.
436.4 Table of contents.
436.5 Disclosure items.

Subpart D—Instructions

436.6 Instructions for preparing disclosure documents.
436.7 Instructions for updating disclosures.

Subpart E—Exemptions

436.8 Exemptions.

Subpart F—Prohibitions

436.9 Additional prohibitions.

Subpart G—Other Provisions

436.10 Other laws and rules.
436.11 Severability.

APPENDIX F TO PART 436—SAMPLE ITEM 20(5) TABLE—PROJECTED NEW FRANCHISED OUTLETS

AUTHORITY: 15 U.S.C. 41-58.

SOURCE: 72 FR 15544, Mar. 30, 2007, unless otherwise noted.

Subpart A—Definitions

§ 436.1 Definitions.

Unless stated otherwise, the following definitions apply throughout part 436:

(a) *Action* includes complaints, cross claims, counterclaims, and third-party complaints in a judicial action or proceeding, and their equivalents in an administrative action or arbitration.

(b) *Affiliate* means an entity controlled by, controlling, or under common control with, another entity.

(c) *Confidentiality clause* means any contract, order, or settlement provision that directly or indirectly restricts a current or former franchisee from discussing his or her personal experience as a franchisee in the franchisor's system with any prospective franchisee. It does not include clauses that protect franchisor's trademarks or other proprietary information.

(d) *Disclose*, *state*, *describe*, and *list* each mean to present all material facts accurately, clearly, concisely, and legibly in plain English.

(e) *Financial performance representation* means any representation, including any oral, written, or visual representation, to a prospective franchisee, including a representation in the general media, that states, expressly or by implication, a specific level or range of actual or potential sales, income, gross profits, or net profits. The term includes a chart, table, or mathematical calculation that shows possible results based on a combination of variables.

(f) *Fiscal year* refers to the franchisor's fiscal year.

(g) *Fractional franchise* means a franchise relationship that satisfies the following criteria when the relationship is created:

(1) The franchisee, any of the franchisee's current directors or officers, or any current directors or officers of a parent or affiliate, has more than two years of experience in the same type of business; and

(2) The parties have a reasonable basis to anticipate that the sales arising from the relationship will not exceed 20% of the franchisee's total dollar volume in sales during the first year of operation.

(h) *Franchise* means any continuing commercial relationship or arrangement, whatever it may be called, in which the terms of the offer or contract specify, or the franchise seller promises or represents, orally or in writing, that:

(1) The franchisee will obtain the right to operate a business that is identified or associated with the franchisor's trademark, or to offer, sell, or distribute goods, services, or commodities that are identified or associated with the franchisor's trademark;

(2) The franchisor will exert or has authority to exert a significant degree of control over the franchisee's method of operation, or provide significant assistance in the franchisee's method of operation; and

(3) As a condition of obtaining or commencing operation of the franchise, the franchisee makes a required payment or commits to make a required payment to the franchisor or its affiliate.

(i) *Franchisee* means any person who is granted a franchise.

(j) *Franchise seller* means a person that offers for sale, sells, or arranges for the sale of a franchise. It includes the franchisor and the franchisor's employees, representatives, agents, subfranchisors, and third-party brokers who are involved in franchise sales activities. It does not include existing franchisees who sell only their own outlet and who are otherwise not engaged in franchise sales on behalf of the franchisor.

(k) *Franchisor* means any person who grants a franchise and participates in the franchise relationship. Unless otherwise stated, it includes subfranchisors. For purposes of this definition, a "subfranchisor" means a person who functions as a franchisor by engaging in both pre-sale activities and post-sale performance.

(l) *Leased department* means an arrangement whereby a retailer licenses or otherwise permits a seller to conduct ≤business from the retailer's location where the seller purchases no goods, services, or commodities directly or indirectly from the retailer, a person the retailer requires the seller to do business with, or a retailer-affiliate if the retailer advises the seller to do business with the affiliate.

(m) *Parent* means an entity that controls another entity directly, or indirectly through one or more subsidiaries.

(n) *Person* means any individual, group, association, limited or general partnership, corporation, or any other entity.

(o) *Plain English* means the organization of information and language usage understandable by a person unfamiliar with the franchise business. It incorporates short sentences; definite, concrete, everyday language; active voice; and tabular presentation of information, where possible. It avoids legal jargon, highly technical business terms, and multiple negatives.

(p) *Predecessor* means a person from whom the franchisor acquired, directly or indirectly, the major portion of the franchisor's assets.

(q) *Principal business address* means the street address of a person's home office in the United States. A principal business address cannot be a post office box or private mail drop.

(r) *Prospective franchisee* means any person (including any agent, representative, or employee) who approaches or is approached by a franchise seller to discuss the possible establishment of a franchise relationship.

(s) *Required payment* means all consideration that the franchisee must pay to the franchisor or an affiliate, either by contract or by practical necessity, as a condition of obtaining or commencing operation of the franchise. A required payment does not include payments for the purchase of reasonable amounts of inventory at bona fide wholesale prices for resale or lease.

(t) *Sale of a franchise* includes an agreement whereby a person obtains a franchise from a franchise seller for value by purchase, license, or otherwise. It does not include extending or renewing an existing franchise agreement where there has been no interruption in the franchisee's operation of the business, unless the new agreement contains terms and conditions that differ materially from the original agreement. It also does not include the transfer of a franchise by an existing franchisee where the franchisor has had no significant involvement with the prospective transferee. A franchisor's approval or disapproval of a transfer alone is not deemed to be significant involvement.

(u) *Signature* means a person's affirmative step to authenticate his or her identity. It includes a person's handwritten signature, as well as a person's use of security codes, passwords, electronic signatures, and similar devices to authenticate his or her identity.

(v) *Trademark* includes trademarks, service marks, names, logos, and other commercial symbols.

(w) *Written* or *in writing* means any document or information in printed form or in any form capable of being preserved in tangible form and read. It includes: type-set, word processed, or handwritten document; information on computer disk or CD-ROM; information sent via email; or information posted on the Internet. It does not include mere oral statements.

Subpart B—Franchisors' Obligations

§436.2 Obligation to furnish documents.

In connection with the offer or sale of a franchise to be located in the United States of America or its territories, unless the transaction is exempted under subpart E of this part, it is an unfair or deceptive act or practice in violation of Section 5 of the Federal Trade Commission Act:

(a) For any franchisor to fail to furnish a prospective franchisee with a copy of the franchisor's current disclosure document, as described in subparts C and D of this part, at least 14 calendar-days before the prospective franchisee signs a binding agreement with, or makes any payment to, the franchisor or an affiliate in connection with the proposed franchise sale.

(b) For any franchisor to alter unilaterally and materially the terms and conditions of the basic franchise agreement or any related agreements attached to the disclosure document without furnishing the prospective franchisee with a copy of each revised agreement at least seven calendar-days before the prospective franchisee signs the revised agreement. Changes to an agreement that arise out of negotiations initiated by the prospective franchisee do not trigger this seven calendar-day period.

(c) For purposes of paragraphs (a) and (b) of this section, the franchisor has furnished the documents by the required date if:

(1) A copy of the document was hand-delivered, faxed, emailed, or otherwise delivered to the prospective franchisee by the required date;

(2) Directions for accessing the document on the Internet were provided to the prospective franchisee by the required date; or

(3) A paper or tangible electronic copy (for example, computer disk or CD-ROM) was sent to the address specified by the prospective franchisee by first-class United States mail at least three calendar days before the required date.

Subpart C—Contents of a Disclosure Document

§ 436.3   Cover page.

Begin the disclosure document with a cover page, in the order and form as follows:

(a) The title "FRANCHISE DISCLOSURE DOCUMENT" in capital letters and bold type.

(b) The franchisor's name, type of business organization, principal business address, telephone number, and, if applicable, email address and primary home page address.

(c) A sample of the primary business trademark that the franchisee will use in its business.

(d) A brief description of the franchised business.

(e) The following statements:

(1) The total investment necessary to begin operation of a [franchise system name] franchise is [the total amount of Item 7 (§ 436.5(g))]. This includes [the total amount in Item 5 (§ 436.5(e))] that must be paid to the franchisor or affiliate.

(2) This disclosure document summarizes certain provisions of your franchise agreement and other information in plain English. Read this disclosure document and all accompanying agreements carefully. You must receive this disclosure document at least 14 calendar-days before you sign a binding agreement with, or make any payment to, the franchisor or an affiliate in connection with the proposed franchise sale. [The following sentence in bold type] NOTE, HOWEVER, THAT NO GOVERNMENTAL AGENCY HAS VERIFIED THE INFORMATION CONTAINED IN THIS DOCUMENT.

(3) The terms of your contract will govern your franchise relationship. Don't rely on the disclosure document alone to understand your contract. Read all of your contract carefully. Show your contract and this disclosure document to an advisor, like a lawyer or an accountant.

(4) Buying a franchise is a complex investment. The information in this disclosure document can help you make up your mind. More information on franchising, such as "*A Consumer's Guide to Buying a Franchise*," which can help you understand how to use this disclosure document, is available from the Federal Trade Commission. You can contact the FTC at 1-877-FTC-HELP or by writing to the FTC at 600 Pennsylvania Avenue, NW., Washington, D.C. 20580. You can also visit the FTC's home page at *www.ftc.gov* for additional information. Call your state agency or visit your public library for other sources of information on franchising.

(5) There may also be laws on franchising in your state. Ask your state agencies about them.

(6) [The issuance date].

(f) A franchisor may include the following statement between the statements set out at paragraphs (e)(2) and (3) of this section: "You may wish to receive your disclosure document in another format that is more convenient for you. To discuss the availability of disclosures in different formats, contact [name or office] at [address] and [telephone number]."

(g) Franchisors may include additional disclosures on the cover page, on a separate cover page, or addendum to comply with state pre-sale disclosure laws.

§436.4 Table of contents.

Include the following table of contents. State the page where each disclosure Item begins. List all exhibits by letter, as shown in the following example.

TABLE OF CONTENTS

1. The Franchisor and any Parents, Predecessors, and Affiliates
2. Business Experience
3. Litigation
4. Bankruptcy
5. Initial Fees
6. Other Fees
7. Estimated Initial Investment
8. Restrictions on Sources of Products and Services
9. Franchisee's Obligations
10. Financing
11. Franchisor's Assistance, Advertising, Computer Systems, and Training
12. Territory
13. Trademarks
14. Patents, Copyrights, and Proprietary Information
15. Obligation to Participate in the Actual Operation of the Franchise Business
16. Restrictions on What the Franchisee May Sell
17. Renewal, Termination, Transfer, and Dispute Resolution
18. Public Figures
19. Financial Performance Representations
20. Outlets and Franchisee Information
21. Financial Statements
22. Contracts
23. Receipts

EXHIBITS

A. Franchise Agreement

§436.5 Disclosure items.

(a) *Item 1: The Franchisor, and any Parents, Predecessors, and Affiliates.* Disclose:

(1) The name and principal business address of the franchisor; any parents; and any affiliates that offer franchises in any line of business or provide products or services to the franchisees of the franchisor.

(2) The name and principal business address of any predecessors during the 10-year period immediately before the close of the franchisor's most recent fiscal year.

(3) The name that the franchisor uses and any names it intends to use to conduct business.

(4) The identity and principal business address of the franchisor's agent for service of process.

(5) The type of business organization used by the franchisor (for example, corporation, partnership) and the state in which it was organized.

(6) The following information about the franchisor's business and the franchises offered:

(i) Whether the franchisor operates businesses of the type being franchised.

(ii) The franchisor's other business activities.

(iii) The business the franchisee will conduct.

(iv) The general market for the product or service the franchisee will offer. In describing the general market, consider factors such as whether the market is developed or developing, whether the goods will be sold primarily to a certain group, and whether sales are seasonal.

(v) In general terms, any laws or regulations specific to the industry in which the franchise business operates.

(vi) A general description of the competition.

(7) The prior business experience of the franchisor; any predecessors listed in §436.5(a)(2) of this part; and any affiliates that offer franchises in any line of business or provide products or services to the franchisees of the franchisor, including:

(i) The length of time each has conducted the type of business the franchisee will operate.

(ii) The length of time each has offered franchises providing the type of business the franchisee will operate.

(iii) Whether each has offered franchises in other lines of business. If so, include:

(A) A description of each other line of business.

(B) The number of franchises sold in each other line of business.

(C) The length of time each has offered franchises in each other line of business.

(b) *Item 2: Business Experience.* Disclose by name and position the franchisor's directors, trustees, general partners, principal officers, and any other individuals who will have management responsibility relating to the sale or operation of franchises offered by this document. For each person listed in this section, state his or her principal positions and employers during the past five years, including each position's starting date, ending date, and location.

(c) *Item 3: Litigation.* (1) Disclose whether the franchisor; a predecessor; a parent or affiliate who induces franchise sales by promising to back the franchisor financially or otherwise guarantees the franchisor's performance; an affiliate who offers franchises under the franchisor's principal trademark; and any person identified in § 436.5(b) of this part:

(i) Has pending against that person:

(A) An administrative, criminal, or material civil action alleging a violation of a franchise, antitrust, or securities law, or alleging fraud, unfair or deceptive practices, or comparable allegations.

(B) Civil actions, other than ordinary routine litigation incidental to the business, which are material in the context of the number of franchisees and the size, nature, or financial condition of the franchise system or its business operations.

(ii) Was a party to any material civil action involving the franchise relationship in the last fiscal year. For purposes of this section, "franchise relationship" means contractual obligations between the franchisor and franchisee directly relating to the operation of the franchised business (such as royalty payment and training obligations). It does not include actions involving suppliers or other third parties, or indemnification for tort liability.

(iii) Has in the 10-year period immediately before the disclosure document's issuance date:

(A) Been convicted of or pleaded nolo contendere to a felony charge.

(B) Been held liable in a civil action involving an alleged violation of a franchise, antitrust, or securities law, or involving allegations of fraud, unfair or deceptive practices, or comparable allegations. "Held liable" means that, as a result of claims or counterclaims, the person must pay money or other consideration, must reduce an indebtedness by the amount of an award, cannot enforce its rights, or must take action adverse to its interests.

(2) Disclose whether the franchisor; a predecessor; a parent or affiliate who guarantees the franchisor's performance; an affiliate who has offered or sold franchises in any line of business within the last 10 years; or any other person identified in § 436.5(b) of this part is subject to a currently effective injunctive or restrictive order or decree resulting from a pending or concluded action brought by a public agency and relating to the franchise or to a Federal, State, or Canadian franchise, securities, antitrust, trade regulation, or trade practice law.

(3) For each action identified in paragraphs (c)(1) and (2) of this section, state the title, case number or citation, the initial filing date, the names of the parties, the forum, and the relationship of the opposing party to the franchisor (for example, competitor, supplier, lessor, franchisee, former franchisee, or class of franchisees). Except as provided in paragraph (c)(4) of this section, summarize the legal and factual nature of each claim in the action, the relief sought or obtained, and any conclusions of law or fact.[1] In addition, state:

(i) For pending actions, the status of the action.

(ii) For prior actions, the date when the judgment was entered and any damages or settlement terms.[2]

(iii) For injunctive or restrictive orders, the nature, terms, and conditions of the order or decree.

-----

[1] Franchisors may include a summary opinion of counsel concerning any action if counsel consent to use the summary opinion and the full opinion is attached to the disclosure document.

[2] If a settlement agreement must be disclosed in this Item, all material settlement terms must be disclosed, whether or not the agreement is confidential. However, franchisors need not disclose the terms of confidential settlements entered into before commencing franchise sales. Further, any franchisor who has historically used only the Franchise Rule format, or who is new to franchising, need not disclose confidential settlements entered prior to the effective date of this Rule.

(iv) For convictions or pleas, the crime or violation, the date of conviction, and the sentence or penalty imposed.

(4) For any other franchisor-initiated suit identified in paragraph (c)(1)(ii) of this section, the franchisor may comply with the requirements of paragraphs (c)(3)(i) through (iv) of this section by listing individual suits under one common heading that will serve as the case summary (for example, "royalty collection suits").

(d) *Item 4: Bankruptcy.* (1) Disclose whether the franchisor; any parent; predecessor; affiliate; officer, or general partner of the franchisor, or any other individual who will have management responsibility relating to the sale or operation of franchises offered by this document, has, during the 10-year period immediately before the date of this disclosure document:

(i) Filed as debtor (or had filed against it) a petition under the United States Bankruptcy Code ("Bankruptcy Code").

(ii) Obtained a discharge of its debts under the Bankruptcy Code.

(iii) Been a principal officer of a company or a general partner in a partnership that either filed as a debtor (or had filed against it) a petition under the Bankruptcy Code, or that obtained a discharge of its debts under the Bankruptcy Code while, or within one year after, the officer or general partner held the position in the company.

(2) For each bankruptcy, state:

(i) The current name, address, and principal place of business of the debtor.

(ii) Whether the debtor is the franchisor. If not, state the relationship of the debtor to the franchisor (for example, affiliate, officer).

(iii) The date of the original filing and the material facts, including the bankruptcy court, and the case name and number. If applicable, state the debtor's discharge date, including discharges under Chapter 7 and confirmation of any plans of reorganization under Chapters 11 and 13 of the Bankruptcy Code.

(3) Disclose cases, actions, and other proceedings under the laws of foreign nations relating to bankruptcy.

(e) *Item 5: Initial Fees.* Disclose the initial fees and any conditions under which these fees are refundable. If the initial fees are not uniform, disclose the range or formula used to calculate the initial fees paid in the fiscal year before the issuance date and the factors that determined the amount. For this section, "initial fees" means all fees and payments, or commitments to pay, for services or goods received from the franchisor or any affiliate before the franchisee's business opens, whether payable in lump sum or installments. Disclose installment payment terms in this section or in §436.5(j) of this part.

(f) *Item 6: Other Fees.* Disclose, in the following tabular form, all other fees that the franchisee must pay to the franchisor or its affiliates, or that the franchisor or its affiliates impose or collect in whole or in part for a third party. State the title "OTHER FEES" in capital letters using bold type. Include any formula used to compute the fees.[3]

ITEM 6 TABLE

OTHER FEES

Column 1 Type of fee	Column 2 Amount	Column 3 Due Date	Column 4 Remarks

(1) In column 1, list the type of fee (for example, royalties, and fees for lease negotiations, construction, remodeling, additional training or assistance, advertising, advertising cooperatives, purchasing cooperatives, audits,

---

[3] If fees may increase, disclose the formula that determines the increase or the maximum amount of the increase. For example, a percentage of gross sales is acceptable if the franchisor defines the term "gross sales."

accounting, inventory, transfers, and renewals).

(2) In column 2, state the amount of the fee.

(3) In column 3, state the due date for each fee.

(4) In column 4, include remarks, definitions, or caveats that elaborate on the information in the table. If remarks are long, franchisors may use footnotes instead of the remarks column. If applicable, include the following information in the remarks column or in a footnote:

(i) Whether the fees are payable only to the franchisor.

(ii) Whether the fees are imposed and collected by the franchisor.

(iii) Whether the fees are non-refundable or describe the circumstances when the fees are refundable.

(iv) Whether the fees are uniformly imposed.

(v) The voting power of franchisor-owned outlets on any fees imposed by cooperatives. If franchisor-owned outlets have controlling voting power, disclose the maximum and minimum fees that may be imposed.

(g) *Item 7: Estimated Initial Investment.* Disclose, in the following tabular form, the franchisee's estimated initial investment. State the title "YOUR ESTIMATED INITIAL INVESTMENT" in capital letters using bold type. Franchisors may include additional expenditure tables to show expenditure variations caused by differences such as in site location and premises size.

ITEM 7 TABLE:
YOUR ESTIMATED INITIAL INVESTMENT

Column 1 Type of expenditure	Column 2 Amount	Column 3 Method of payment	Column 4 When due	Column 4 To whom payment is to be made
Total.				

(1) In column 1:

(i) List each type of expense, beginning with pre-opening expenses. Include the following expenses, if applicable. Use footnotes to include remarks, definitions, or caveats that elaborate on the information in the Table.

(A) The initial franchise fee.

(B) Training expenses.

(C) Real property, whether purchased or leased.

(D) Equipment, fixtures, other fixed assets, construction, remodeling, leasehold improvements, and decorating costs, whether purchased or leased.

(E) Inventory to begin operating.

(F) Security deposits, utility deposits, business licenses, and other prepaid expenses.

(ii) List separately and by name any other specific required payments (for example, additional training, travel, or advertising expenses) that the franchisee must make to begin operations.

(iii) Include a category titled "Additional funds— [initial period]" for any other required expenses the franchisee will incur before operations begin and during the initial period of operations. State the initial period. A reasonable initial period is at least three months or a reasonable period for the industry. Describe in general terms the factors, basis, and experience that the franchisor considered or relied upon in formulating the amount required for additional funds.

(2) In column 2, state the amount of the payment. If the amount is unknown, use a low-high range based on the franchisor's current experience. If real property costs cannot be estimated in a low-high range, describe the approximate size of the property and building and the probable location of the building (for example, strip shopping center, mall, downtown, rural, or highway).

(3) In column 3, state the method of payment.

(4) In column 4, state the due date.

(5) In column 5, state to whom payment will be made.

(6) Total the initial investment, incorporating ranges of fees, if used.

(7) In a footnote, state:

(i) Whether each payment is non-refundable, or describe the circumstances when each payment is refundable.

(ii) If the franchisor or an affiliate finances part of the initial investment, the amount that it will finance, the required down payment, the annual interest rate, rate factors, and the estimated loan repayments. Franchisors may refer to §436.5(j) of this part for additional details.

(h) *Item 8: Restrictions on Sources of Products and Services.* Disclose the franchisee's obligations to purchase or lease goods, services, supplies, fixtures, equipment, inventory, computer hardware and software, real estate, or comparable items related to establishing or operating the franchised business either from the franchisor, its designee, or suppliers approved by the franchisor, or under the franchisor's specifications. Include obligations to purchase imposed by the franchisor's written agreement or by the franchisor's practice.[4] For each applicable obligation, state:

(1) The good or service required to be purchased or leased.

(2) Whether the franchisor or its affiliates are approved suppliers or the only approved suppliers of that good or service.

(3) Any supplier in which an officer of the franchisor owns an interest.

(4) How the franchisor grants and revokes approval of alternative suppliers, including:

(i) Whether the franchisor's criteria for approving suppliers are available to franchisees.

(ii) Whether the franchisor permits franchisees to contract with alternative suppliers who meet the franchisor's criteria.

(iii) Any fees and procedures to secure approval to purchase from alternative suppliers.

(iv) The time period in which the franchisee will be notified of approval or disapproval.

(v) How approvals are revoked.

(5) Whether the franchisor issues specifications and standards to franchisees, subfranchisees, or approved suppliers. If so, describe how the franchisor issues and modifies specifications.

(6) Whether the franchisor or its affiliates will or may derive revenue or other material consideration from required purchases or leases by franchisees. If so, describe the precise basis by which the franchisor or its affiliates will or may derive that consideration by stating:

(i) The franchisor's total revenue.[5]

(ii) The franchisor's revenues from all required purchases and leases of products and services.

(iii) The percentage of the franchisor's total revenues that are from required purchases or leases.

(iv) If the franchisor's affiliates also sell or lease products or services to franchisees, the affiliates' revenues from those sales or leases.

(7) The estimated proportion of these required purchases and leases by the franchisee to all purchases and leases by the franchisee of goods and services in establishing and operating the franchised businesses.

(8) If a designated supplier will make payments to the franchisor from franchisee purchases, disclose the basis for the payment (for example, specify a percentage or a flat amount). For purposes of this disclosure, a "payment" includes the sale of similar goods or services to the franchisor at a lower price than to franchisees.

(9) The existence of purchasing or distribution cooperatives.

---

[4] Franchisors may include the reason for the requirement. Franchisors need not disclose in this Item the purchase or lease of goods or services provided as part of the franchise without a separate charge (such as initial training, if the cost is included in the franchise fee). Describe such fees in Item 5 of this section. Do not disclose fees already described in §436.5(f) of this part.

[5] Take figures from the franchisor's most recent annual audited financial statement required in §436.5(u) of this part. If audited statements are not yet required, or if the entity deriving the income is an affiliate, disclose the sources of information used in computing revenues.

(10) Whether the franchisor negotiates purchase arrangements with suppliers, including price terms, for the benefit of franchisees.

(11) Whether the franchisor provides material benefits (for example, renewal or granting additional franchises) to a franchisee based on a franchisee's purchase of particular products or services or use of particular suppliers.

(i) *Item 9: Franchisee's Obligations.* Disclose, in the following tabular form, a list of the franchisee's principal obligations. State the title "FRANCHISEE'S OBLIGATIONS" in capital letters using bold type. Cross-reference each listed obligation with any applicable section of the franchise or other agreement and with the relevant disclosure document provision. If a particular obligation is not applicable, state "Not Applicable." Include additional obligations, as warranted.

ITEM 9 TABLE:
FRANCHISEE'S OBLIGATIONS

[In bold] **This table lists your principal obligations under the franchise and other agreements. It will help you find more detailed information about your obligations in these agreements and in other items of this disclosure document.**

Obligation	Section in agreement	Disclosure document item
a. Site selection and acquisition/lease		
b. Pre-opening purchase/leases		
c. Site development and other pre-opening requirements		
d. Initial and ongoing training		
e. Opening		
f. Fees		
g. Compliance with standards and policies/operating manual		
h. Trademarks and proprietary information		
i. Restrictions on products/services offered		
j. Warranty and customer service requirements		
k. Territorial development and sales quotas		
l. Ongoing product/service purchases		
m. Maintenance, appearance, and remodeling requirements		
n. Insurance		
o. Advertising		
p. Indemnification		
q. Owner's participation/management/staffing		
r. Records and reports		
s. Inspections and audits		
t. Transfer		
u. Renewal		
v. Post-termination obligations		
w. Non-competition covenants		
x. Dispute resolution		
y. Other (describe)		

(j) *Item 10*: *Financing.* (1) Disclose the terms of each financing arrangement, including leases and installment contracts, that the franchisor, its agent, or affiliates offer directly or indirectly to the franchisee.[6] The franchisor may summarize the terms of each financing arrangement in tabular form, using footnotes to provide additional information. For a sample Item 10 table, see appendix A of this part. For each financing arrangement, state:

(i) What the financing covers (for example, the initial franchise fee, site acquisition, construction or remodeling, initial or replacement equipment or fixtures, opening or ongoing inventory or supplies, or other continuing expenses).[7]

(ii) The identity of each lender providing financing and their relationship to the franchisor (for example, affiliate).

(iii) The amount of financing offered or, if the amount depends on an actual cost that may vary, the percentage of the cost that will be financed.

(iv) The rate of interest, plus finance charges, expressed on an annual basis. If the rate of interest, plus finance charges, expressed on an annual basis, may differ depending on when the financing is issued, state what that rate was on a specified recent date.

(v) The number of payments or the period of repayment.

(vi) The nature of any security interest required by the lender.

(vii) Whether a person other than the franchisee must personally guarantee the debt.

(viii) Whether the debt can be prepaid and the nature of any prepayment penalty.

(ix) The franchisee's potential liabilities upon default, including any:

------

[6] Indirect offers of financing include a written arrangement between a franchisor or its affiliate and a lender, for the lender to offer financing to a franchisee; an arrangement in which a franchisor or its affiliate receives a benefit from a lender in exchange for financing a franchise purchase; and a franchisor's guarantee of a note, lease, or other obligation of the franchisee.

[7] Include sample copies of the financing documents as an exhibit to §436.5(v) of this part. Cite the section and name of the document containing the financing terms and conditions.

(A) Accelerated obligation to pay the entire amount due;

(B) Obligations to pay court costs and attorney's fees incurred in collecting the debt;

(C) Termination of the franchise; and

(D) Liabilities from cross defaults such as those resulting directly from non-payment, or indirectly from the loss of business property.

(x) Other material financing terms.

(2) Disclose whether the loan agreement requires franchisees to waive defenses or other legal rights (for example, confession of judgment), or bars franchisees from asserting a defense against the lender, the lender's assignee or the franchisor. If so, describe the relevant provisions.

(3) Disclose whether the franchisor's practice or intent is to sell, assign, or discount to a third party all or part of the financing arrangement. If so, state:

(i) The assignment terms, including whether the franchisor will remain primarily obligated to provide the financed goods or services; and

(ii) That the franchisee may lose all its defenses against the lender as a result of the sale or assignment.

(4) Disclose whether the franchisor or an affiliate receives any consideration for placing financing with the lender. If such payments exist:

(i) Disclose the amount or the method of determining the payment; and

(ii) Identify the source of the payment and the relationship of the source to the franchisor or its affiliates.

(k) *Item 11: Franchisor's Assistance, Advertising, Computer Systems, and Training.* Disclose the franchisor's principal assistance and related obligations of both the franchisor and franchisee as follows. For each obligation, cite the section number of the franchise agreement imposing the obligation. Begin by stating the following sentence in bold type: "EXCEPT AS LISTED BELOW, [THE FRANCHISOR] IS NOT REQUIRED TO PROVIDE YOU WITH ANY ASSISTANCE."

(1) Disclose the franchisor's pre-opening obligations to the franchisee, including any assistance in:

(i) Locating a site and negotiating the purchase or lease of the site. If such assistance is provided, state:

(A) Whether the franchisor generally owns the premises and leases it to the franchisee.

(B) Whether the franchisor selects the site or approves an area in which the franchisee selects a site. If so, state further whether and how the franchisor must approve a franchisee-selected site.

(C) The factors that the franchisor considers in selecting or approving sites (for example, general location and neighborhood, traffic patterns, parking, size, physical characteristics of existing buildings, and lease terms).

(D) The time limit for the franchisor to locate or approve or disapprove the site and the consequences if the franchisor and franchisee cannot agree on a site.

(ii) Conforming the premises to local ordinances and building codes and obtaining any required permits.

(iii) Constructing, remodeling, or decorating the premises.

(iv) Hiring and training employees.

(v) Providing for necessary equipment, signs, fixtures, opening inventory, and supplies. If any such assistance is provided, state:

(A) Whether the franchisor provides these items directly or only provides the names of approved suppliers.

(B) Whether the franchisor provides written specifications for these items.

(C) Whether the franchisor delivers or installs these items.

(2) Disclose the typical length of time between the earlier of the signing of the franchise agreement or the first payment of consideration for the franchise and the opening of the franchisee's business. Describe the factors that may affect the time period, such as ability to obtain a lease, financing or building permits, zoning and local ordinances, weather conditions, shortages, or delayed installation of equipment, fixtures, and signs.

(3) Disclose the franchisor's obligations to the franchisee during the operation of the franchise, including any assistance in:

(i) Developing products or services the franchisee will offer to its customers.

(ii) Hiring and training employees.

(iii) Improving and developing the franchised business.

(iv) Establishing prices.

(v) Establishing and using administrative, bookkeeping, accounting, and inventory control procedures.

(vi) Resolving operating problems encountered by the franchisee.

(4) Describe the advertising program for the franchise system, including the following:

(i) The franchisor's obligation to conduct advertising, including:

(A) The media the franchisor may use.

(B) Whether media coverage is local, regional, or national.

(C) The source of the advertising (for example, an in-house advertising department or a national or regional advertising agency).

(D) Whether the franchisor must spend any amount on advertising in the area or territory where the franchisee is located.

(ii) The circumstances when the franchisor will permit franchisees to use their own advertising material.

(iii) Whether there is an advertising council composed of franchisees that advises the franchisor on advertising policies. If so, disclose:

(A) How members of the council are selected.

(B) Whether the council serves in an advisory capacity only or has operational or decision-making power.

(C) Whether the franchisor has the power to form, change, or dissolve the advertising council.

(iv) Whether the franchisee must participate in a local or regional advertising cooperative. If so, state:

(A) How the area or membership of the cooperative is defined.

(B) How much the franchisee must contribute to the fund and whether other franchisees must contribute a different amount or at a different rate.

(C) Whether the franchisor-owned outlets must contribute to the fund and, if so, whether those contributions are on the same basis as those for franchisees.

(D) Who is responsible for administering the cooperative (for example, franchisor, franchisees, or advertising agency).

(E) Whether cooperatives must operate from written governing documents and whether the documents are available for the franchisee to review.

(F) Whether cooperatives must prepare annual or periodic financial statements and whether the statements are available for review by the franchisee.

(G) Whether the franchisor has the power to require cooperatives to be formed, changed, dissolved, or merged.

(v) Whether the franchisee must participate in any other advertising fund. If so, state:

(A) Who contributes to the fund.

(B) How much the franchisee must contribute to the fund and whether other franchisees must contribute a different amount or at a different rate.

(C) Whether the franchisor-owned outlets must contribute to the fund and, if so, whether it is on the same basis as franchisees.

(D) Who administers the fund.

(E) Whether the fund is audited and when it is audited.

(F) Whether financial statements of the fund are available for review by the franchisee.

(G) How the funds were used in the most recently concluded fiscal year, including the percentages spent on production, media placement, administrative expenses, and a description of any other use.

(vi) If not all advertising funds are spent in the fiscal year in which they accrue, how the franchisor uses the remaining amount, including whether franchisees receive a periodic accounting of how advertising fees are spent.

(vii) The percentage of advertising funds, if any, that the franchisor uses principally to solicit new franchise sales.

(5) Disclose whether the franchisor requires the franchisee to buy or use electronic cash registers or computer systems. If so, describe the systems generally in non-technical language, including the types of data to be generated or stored in these systems, and state the following:

(i) The cost of purchasing or leasing the systems.

(ii) Any obligation of the franchisor, any affiliate, or third party to provide ongoing maintenance, repairs, upgrades, or updates.

(iii) Any obligations of the franchisee to upgrade or update any system during the term of the franchise, and, if so, any contractual limitations on the frequency and cost of the obligation.

(iv) The annual cost of any optional or required maintenance, updating, upgrading, or support contracts.

(v) Whether the franchisor will have independent access to the information that will be generated or stored in any electronic cash register or computer system. If so, describe the information that the franchisor may access and whether there are any contractual limitations on the franchisor's right to access the information.

(6) Disclose the table of contents of the franchisor's operating manual provided to franchisees as of the franchisor's last fiscal year-end or a more recent date. State the number of pages devoted to each subject and the total number of pages in the manual as of this date. This disclosure may be omitted if the franchisor offers the prospective franchisee the opportunity to view the manual before buying the franchise.

(7) Disclose the franchisor's training program as of the franchisor's last fiscal year-end or a more recent date.

(i) Describe the training program in the following tabular form. Title the table "TRAINING PROGRAM" in capital letters and bold type.

ITEM 11 TABLE
TRAINING PROGRAM

Column 1 Subject	Column 2 Hours of Classroom Training	Column 3 Hours of On-The-Job Training	Column 4 Location

(A) In column 1, state the subjects taught.

(B) In column 2, state the hours of classroom training for each subject.

(C) In column 3, state the hours of on-the-job training for each subject.

(D) In column 4, state the location of the training for each subject.

(ii) State further:

(A) How often training classes are held and the nature of the location or facility where training is held (for example, company, home, office, franchisor-owned store).

(B) The nature of instructional materials and the instructor's experience, including the instructor's length of experience in the field and with the franchisor. State only experience relevant to the subject taught and the franchisor's operations.

(C) Any charges franchisees must pay for training and who must pay travel and living expenses of the training program enrollees.

(D) Who may and who must attend training. State whether the franchisee or other persons must complete the program to the franchisor's satisfaction. If successful completion is required, state how long after signing the agreement or before opening the business the training must be completed. If training is not mandatory, state the percentage of new franchisees that enrolled in the training program during the preceding 12 months.

(E) Whether additional training programs or refresher courses are required.

(l) *Item 12: Territory.* Disclose:

(1) Whether the franchise is for a specific location or a location to be approved by the franchisor.

(2) Any minimum territory granted to the franchisee (for example, a specific radius, a distance sufficient to encompass a specified population, or another specific designation).

(3) The conditions under which the franchisor will approve the relocation of the franchised business or the franchisee's establishment of additional franchised outlets.

(4) Franchisee options, rights of first refusal, or similar rights to acquire additional franchises.

(5) Whether the franchisor grants an exclusive territory.

(i) If the franchisor does not grant an exclusive territory, state: "You will not receive an exclusive territory. You may face competition from other franchisees, from outlets that we own, or from other channels of distribution or competitive brands that we control."

(ii) If the franchisor grants an exclusive territory, disclose:

(A) Whether continuation of territorial exclusivity depends on achieving a certain sales volume, market penetration, or other contingency, and the circumstances when the franchisee's territory may be altered. Describe any sales or other conditions. State the franchisor's rights if the franchisee fails to meet the requirements.

(B) Any other circumstances that permit the franchisor to modify the franchisee's territorial rights (for example, a population increase in the territory giving the franchisor the right to grant an additional franchise in the area) and the effect of such modifications on the franchisee's rights.

(6) For all territories (exclusive and non-exclusive):

(i) Any restrictions on the franchisor from soliciting or accepting orders from consumers inside the franchisee's territory, including:

(A) Whether the franchisor or an affiliate has used or reserves the right to use other channels of distribution, such as the Internet, catalog sales, telemarketing, or other direct marketing sales, to make sales within the franchisee's territory using the franchisor's principal trademarks.

(B) Whether the franchisor or an affiliate has used or reserves the right to use other channels of distribution, such as the Internet, catalog sales, telemarketing, or other direct marketing, to make sales within the franchisee's territory of products or services under trademarks different from the ones the franchisee will use under the franchise agreement.

(C) Any compensation that the franchisor must pay for soliciting or accepting orders from inside the franchisee's territory.

(ii) Any restrictions on the franchisee from soliciting or accepting orders from consumers outside of his or her territory, including whether the franchisee has the right to use other channels of distribution, such as the Internet, catalog sales, telemarketing, or other direct marketing, to make sales outside of his or her territory.

(iii) If the franchisor or an affiliate operates, franchises, or has plans to operate or franchise a business under a different trademark and that business sells or will sell goods or services similar to those the franchisee will offer, describe:

(A) The similar goods and services.

(B) The different trademark.

(C) Whether outlets will be franchisor owned or operated.

(D) Whether the franchisor or its franchisees who use the different trademark will solicit or accept orders within the franchisee's territory.

(E) The timetable for the plan.

(F) How the franchisor will resolve conflicts between the franchisor and franchisees and between the franchisees of each system regarding territory, customers, and franchisor support.

(G) The principal business address of the franchisor's similar operating business. If it is the same as the franchisor's principal business address stated in § 436.5(a) of this part, disclose whether the franchisor maintains (or plans to maintain) physically separate offices and training facilities for the similar competing business.

(m) *Item 13: Trademarks.* (1) Disclose each principal trademark to be licensed to the franchisee. For this Item, "principal trademark" means the primary trademarks, service marks, names, logos, and commercial symbols the franchisee will use to identify the franchised business. It may not include every trademark the franchisor owns.

(2) Disclose whether each principal trademark is registered with the United States Patent and Trademark Office. If so, state:

(i) The date and identification number of each trademark registration.

(ii) Whether the franchisor has filed all required affidavits.

(iii) Whether any registration has been renewed.

(iv) Whether the principal trademarks are registered on the Principal or Supplemental Register of the United States Patent and Trademark Office.

(3) If the principal trademark is not registered with the United States Patent and Trademark Office, state whether the franchisor has filed any trademark application, including any "intent to use" application or an application based on actual use. If so, state the date and identification number of the application.

(4) If the trademark is not registered on the Principal Register of the United States Patent and Trademark Office, state: "We do not have a federal registration for our principal trademark. Therefore, our trademark does not have many legal benefits and rights as a federally registered trademark. If our right to use the trademark is challenged, you may have to change to an alternative trademark, which may increase your expenses."

(5) Disclose any currently effective material determinations of the United States Patent and Trademark Office, the Trademark Trial and Appeal Board, or any state trademark administrator or court; and any pending infringement, opposition, or cancellation proceeding. Include infringement, opposition, or cancellation proceedings in which the franchisor unsuccessfully sought to prevent registration of a trademark in order to protect a trademark licensed by the franchisor. Describe how the determination affects the ownership, use, or licensing of the trademark.

(6) Disclose any pending material federal or state court litigation regarding the franchisor's use or ownership rights in a trademark. For each pending action, disclose:[8]

(i) The forum and case number.

(ii) The nature of claims made opposing the franchisor's use of the trademark or by the franchisor opposing another person's use of the trademark.

(iii) Any effective court or administrative agency ruling in the matter.

(7) Disclose any currently effective agreements that significantly limit the franchisor's rights to use or license the use of trademarks listed in this section

---

[8] The franchisor may include an attorney's opinion relative to the merits of litigation or of an action if the attorney issuing the opinion consents to its use. The text of the disclosure may include a summary of the opinion if the full opinion is attached and the attorney issuing the opinion consents to the use of the summary.

in a manner material to the franchise. For each agreement, disclose:

(i) The manner and extent of the limitation or grant.

(ii) The extent to which the agreement may affect the franchisee.

(iii) The agreement's duration.

(iv) The parties to the agreement.

(v) The circumstances when the agreement may be canceled or modified.

(vi) All other material terms.

(8) Disclose:

(i) Whether the franchisor must protect the franchisee's right to use the principal trademarks listed in this section, and must protect the franchisee against claims of infringement or unfair competition arising out of the franchisee's use of the trademarks.

(ii) The franchisee's obligation to notify the franchisor of the use of, or claims of rights to, a trademark identical to or confusingly similar to a trademark licensed to the franchisee.

(iii) Whether the franchise agreement requires the franchisor to take affirmative action when notified of these uses or claims.

(iv) Whether the franchisor or franchisee has the right to control any administrative proceedings or litigation involving a trademark licensed by the franchisor to the franchisee.

(v) Whether the franchise agreement requires the franchisor to participate in the franchisee's defense and/or indemnify the franchisee for expenses or damages if the franchisee is a party to an administrative or judicial proceeding involving a trademark licensed by the franchisor to the franchisee, or if the proceeding is resolved unfavorably to the franchisee.

(vi) The franchisee's rights under the franchise agreement if the franchisor requires the franchisee to modify or discontinue using a trademark.

(9) Disclose whether the franchisor knows of either superior prior rights or infringing uses that could materially affect the franchisee's use of the principal trademarks in the state where the franchised business will be located. For each use of a principal trademark that the franchisor believes is an infringement that could materially affect the franchisee's use of a trademark, disclose:

(i) The nature of the infringement.

(ii) The locations where the infringement is occurring.

(iii) The length of time of the infringement (to the extent known).

(iv) Any action taken or anticipated by the franchisor.

(n) *Item 14: Patents, Copyrights, and Proprietary Information.* (1) Disclose whether the franchisor owns rights in, or licenses to, patents or copyrights that are material to the franchise. Also, disclose whether the franchisor has any pending patent applications that are material to the franchise. If so, state:

(i) The nature of the patent, patent application, or copyright and its relationship to the franchise.

(ii) For each patent:

(A) The duration of the patent.

(B) The type of patent (for example, mechanical, process, or design).

(C) The patent number, issuance date, and title.

(iii) For each patent application:

(A) The type of patent application (for example, mechanical, process, or design).

(B) The serial number, filing date, and title.

(iv) For each copyright:

(A) The duration of the copyright.

(B) The registration number and date.

(C) Whether the franchisor can and intends to renew the copyright.

(2) Describe any current material determination of the United States Patent and Trademark Office, the United States Copyright Office, or a court regarding the patent or copyright. Include the forum and matter number. Describe how the determination affects the franchised business.

(3) State the forum, case number, claims asserted, issues involved, and effective determinations for any material proceeding pending in the United States Patent and Trademark Office or any court.[9]

(4) If an agreement limits the use of the patent, patent application, or copyright, state the parties to and duration of the agreement, the extent to which the agreement may affect the

---

[9] If counsel consents, the franchisor may include a counsel's opinion or a summary of the opinion if the full opinion is attached.

franchisee, and other material terms of the agreement.

(5) Disclose the franchisor's obligation to protect the patent, patent application, or copyright; and to defend the franchisee against claims arising from the franchisee's use of patented or copyrighted items, including:

(i) Whether the franchisor's obligation is contingent upon the franchisee notifying the franchisor of any infringement claims or whether the franchisee's notification is discretionary.

(ii) Whether the franchise agreement requires the franchisor to take affirmative action when notified of infringement.

(iii) Who has the right to control any litigation.

(iv) Whether the franchisor must participate in the defense of a franchisee or indemnify the franchisee for expenses or damages in a proceeding involving a patent, patent application, or copyright licensed to the franchisee.

(v) Whether the franchisor's obligation is contingent upon the franchisee modifying or discontinuing the use of the subject matter covered by the patent or copyright.

(vi) The franchisee's rights under the franchise agreement if the franchisor requires the franchisee to modify or discontinue using the subject matter covered by the patent or copyright.

(6) If the franchisor knows of any patent or copyright infringement that could materially affect the franchisee, disclose:

(i) The nature of the infringement.

(ii) The locations where the infringement is occurring.

(iii) The length of time of the infringement (to the extent known).

(iv) Any action taken or anticipated by the franchisor.

(7) If the franchisor claims proprietary rights in other confidential information or trade secrets, describe in general terms the proprietary information communicated to the franchisee and the terms for use by the franchisee. The franchisor need only describe the general nature of the proprietary information, such as whether a formula or recipe is considered to be a trade secret.

(o) *Item 15: Obligation to Participate in the Actual Operation of the Franchise Business.* (1) Disclose the franchisee's obligation to participate personally in the direct operation of the franchisee's business and whether the franchisor recommends participation. Include obligations arising from any written agreement or from the franchisor's practice.

(2) If personal "on-premises" supervision is not required, disclose the following:

(i) If the franchisee is an individual, whether the franchisor recommends on-premises supervision by the franchisee.

(ii) Limits on whom the franchisee can hire as an on-premises supervisor.

(iii) Whether an on-premises supervisor must successfully complete the franchisor's training program.

(iv) If the franchisee is a business entity, the amount of equity interest, if any, that the on-premises supervisor must have in the franchisee's business.

(3) Disclose any restrictions that the franchisee must place on its manager (for example, maintain trade secrets, covenants not to compete).

(p) *Item 16: Restrictions on What the Franchisee May Sell.* Disclose any franchisor-imposed restrictions or conditions on the goods or services that the franchisee may sell or that limit access to customers, including:

(1) Any obligation on the franchisee to sell only goods or services approved by the franchisor.

(2) Any obligation on the franchisee to sell all goods or services authorized by the franchisor.

(3) Whether the franchisor has the right to change the types of authorized goods or services and whether there are limits on the franchisor's right to make changes.

(q) *Item 17: Renewal, Termination, Transfer, and Dispute Resolution.* Disclose, in the following tabular form, a table that cross-references each enumerated franchise relationship item with the applicable provision in the franchise or related agreement. Title the table "THE FRANCHISE RELATIONSHIP" in capital letters and bold type.

(1) Describe briefly each contractual provision. If a particular item is not applicable, state "Not Applicable."

(2) If the agreement is silent about one of the listed provisions, but the franchisor unilaterally offers to provide certain benefits or protections to franchisees as a matter of policy, use a footnote to describe the policy and state whether the policy is subject to change.

(3) In the summary column for Item 17(c), state what the term "renewal" means for your franchise system, including, if applicable, a statement that franchisees may be asked to sign a contract with materially different terms and conditions than their original contract.

ITEM 17 TABLE:
THE FRANCHISE RELATIONSHIP
[In bold] **This table lists certain important provisions of the franchise and related agreements. You should read these provisions in the agreements attached to this disclosure document.**

Provision	Section in franchise or other agreement	Summary
a. Length of the franchise term		
b. Renewal or extension of the term		
c. Requirements for franchisee to renew or extend		
d. Termination by franchisee		
e. Termination by franchisor without cause		
f. Termination by franchisor with cause		
g. "Cause" defined—curable defaults		
h. "Cause" defined—non-curable defaults		
i. Franchisee's obligations on termination/non-renewal		
j. Assignment of contract by franchisor		
k. "Transfer" by franchisee—defined		
l. Franchisor approval of transfer by franchisee		
m. Conditions for franchisor approval of transfer		
n. Franchisor's right of first refusal to acquire franchisee's business		
o. Franchisor's option to purchase franchisee's business		
p. Death or disability of franchisee		
q. Non-competition covenants during the term of the franchise		
r. Non-competition covenants after the franchise is terminated or expires		
s. Modification of the agreement		
t. Integration/merger clause		
u. Dispute resolution by arbitration or mediation		
v. Choice of forum		
w. Choice of law		

(r) *Item 18: Public Figures.* Disclose:

(1) Any compensation or other benefit given or promised to a public figure arising from either the use of the public figure in the franchise name or symbol, or the public figure's endorsement or recommendation of the franchise to prospective franchisees.

(2) The extent to which the public figure is involved in the management or control of the franchisor. Describe the public figure's position and duties in the franchisor's business structure.

(3) The public figure's total investment in the franchisor, including the amount the public figure contributed in services performed or to be performed. State the type of investment (for example, common stock, promissory note).

(4) For purposes of this section, a public figure means a person whose name or physical appearance is generally known to the public in the geographic area where the franchise will be located.

(s) *Item 19: Financial Performance Representations.* (1) Begin by stating the following:

> The FTC's Franchise Rule permits a franchisor to provide information about the actual or potential financial performance of its franchised and/or franchisor-owned outlets, if there is a reasonable basis for the information, and if the information is included in the disclosure document. Financial performance information that differs from that included in Item 19 may be given only if: (1) a franchisor provides the actual records of an existing outlet you are considering buying; or (2) a franchisor supplements the information provided in this Item 19, for example, by providing information about possible performance at a particular location or under particular circumstances.

(2) If a franchisor does not provide any financial performance representation in Item 19, also state:

> We do not make any representations about a franchisee's future financial performance or the past financial performance of company-owned or franchised outlets. We also do not authorize our employees or representatives to make any such representations either orally or in writing. If you are purchasing an existing outlet, however, we may provide you with the actual records of that outlet. If you receive any other financial performance information or projections of your future income, you should report it to the franchisor's management by contacting [name, address, and telephone number], the Federal Trade Commission, and the appropriate state regulatory agencies.

(3) If the franchisor makes any financial performance representation to prospective franchisees, the franchisor must have a reasonable basis and written substantiation for the representation at the time the representation is made and must state the representation in the Item 19 disclosure. The franchisor must also disclose the following:

(i) Whether the representation is an historic financial performance representation about the franchise system's existing outlets, or a subset of those outlets, or is a forecast of the prospective franchisee's future financial performance.

(ii) If the representation relates to past performance of the franchise system's existing outlets, the material bases for the representation, including:

(A) Whether the representation relates to the performance of all of the franchise system's existing outlets or only to a subset of outlets that share a particular set of characteristics (for example, geographic location, type of location (such as free standing vs. shopping center), degree of competition, length of time the outlets have operated, services or goods sold, services supplied by the franchisor, and whether the outlets are franchised or franchisor-owned or operated).

(B) The dates when the reported level of financial performance was achieved.

(C) The total number of outlets that existed in the relevant period and, if different, the number of outlets that had the described characteristics.

(D) The number of outlets with the described characteristics whose actual financial performance data were used in arriving at the representation.

(E) Of those outlets whose data were used in arriving at the representation, the number and percent that actually attained or surpassed the stated results.

(F) Characteristics of the included outlets, such as those characteristics noted in paragraph (3)(ii)(A) of this section, that may differ materially from those of the outlet that may be offered to a prospective franchisee.

(iii) If the representation is a forecast of future financial performance, state the material bases and assumptions on which the projection is based.

The material assumptions underlying a forecast include significant factors upon which a franchisee's future results are expected to depend. These factors include, for example, economic or market conditions that are basic to a franchisee's operation, and encompass matters affecting, among other things, a franchisee's sales, the cost of goods or services sold, and operating expenses.

(iv) A clear and conspicuous admonition that a new franchisee's individual financial results may differ from the result stated in the financial performance representation.

(v) A statement that written substantiation for the financial performance representation will be made available to the prospective franchisee upon reasonable request.

(4) If a franchisor wishes to disclose only the actual operating results for a specific outlet being offered for sale, it need not comply with this section, provided the information is given only to potential purchasers of that outlet.

(5) If a franchisor furnishes financial performance information according to this section, the franchisor may deliver to a prospective franchisee a supplemental financial performance representation about a particular location or variation, apart from the disclosure document. The supplemental representation must:

(i) Be in writing.

(ii) Explain the departure from the financial performance representation in the disclosure document.

(iii) Be prepared in accordance with the requirements of paragraph (s)(3)(i)-(iv) of this section.

(iv) Be furnished to the prospective franchisee.

(t) *Item 20: Outlets and Franchisee Information.* (1) Disclose, in the following tabular form, the total number of franchised and company-owned outlets for each of the franchisor's last three fiscal years. For purposes of this section, "outlet" includes outlets of a type substantially similar to that offered to the prospective franchisee. A sample Item 20(1) Table is attached as appendix B to this part.

ITEM 20 TABLE NO. 1

Systemwide Outlet Summary

For years [   ] to [   ]

Column 1 Outlet Type	Column 2 Year	Column 3 Outlets at the Start of the Year	Column 4 Outlets at the End of the Year	Column 5 Net Change
Franchised	2004			
	2005			
	2006			
Company-Owned	2004			
	2005			
	2006			
Total Outlets	2004			
	2005			
	2006			

(i) In column 1, include three outlet categories titled "franchised," "company-owned, and "total outlets."

(ii) In column 2, state the last three fiscal years.

(iii) In column 3, state the total number of each type of outlet operating at the beginning of each fiscal year.

(iv) In column 4, state the total number of each type of outlet operating at the end of each fiscal year.

(v) In column 5, state the net change, and indicate whether the change is positive or negative, for each type of outlet during each fiscal year.

(2) Disclose, in the following tabular form, the number of franchised and company-owned outlets and changes in the number and ownership of outlets located in each state during each of the last three fiscal years. Except as noted, each change in ownership shall be reported only once in the following tables. If multiple events occurred in the process of transferring ownership of an outlet, report the event that occurred last in time. If a single outlet changed ownership two or more times during the same fiscal year, use footnotes to describe the types of changes involved and the order in which the changes occurred.

(i) Disclose, in the following tabular form, the total number of franchised outlets transferred in each state during each of the franchisor's last three fiscal years. For purposes of this section, "transfer" means the acquisition of a controlling interest in a franchised outlet, during its term, by a person other than the franchisor or an affiliate. A sample Item 20(2) Table is attached as appendix C to this part.

ITEM 20 TABLE NO. 2

Transfers of Outlets from Franchisees to New Owners (other than the Franchisor)
For years [   ] to [   ]

Column 1 State	Column 2 Year	Column 3 Number of Transfers
	2004	
	2005	
	2006	
	2004	
	2005	
	2006	
Total	2004	
	2005	
	2006	

(A) In column 1, list each state with one or more franchised outlets.

(B) In column 2, state the last three fiscal years.

(C) In column 3, state the total number of completed transfers in each state during each fiscal year.

(ii) Disclose, in the following tabular form, the status of franchisee-owned outlets located in each state for each of the franchisor's last three fiscal years. A sample Item 20(3) Table is attached as appendix D to this part.

ITEM 20 TABLE NO. 3

Status of Franchised Outlets
For years [   ] to [   ]

Column 1 State	Column 2 Year	Column 3 Outlets at Start of Year	Column 4 Outlets Opened	Column 5 Terminations	Column 6 Non-Renewals	Column 7 Reacquired by Franchisor	Column 8 Ceased Operations-Other Reasons	Column 9 Outlets at End of the Year
	2004							
	2005							
	2006							
	2004							
	2005							
	2006							
Totals	2004							
	2005							
	2006							

(A) In column 1, list each state with one or more franchised outlets.

(B) In column 2, state the last three fiscal years.

(C) In column 3, state the total number of franchised outlets in each state at the start of each fiscal year.

(D) In column 4, state the total number of franchised outlets opened in each state during each fiscal year. Include both new outlets and existing company-owned outlets that a franchisee purchased from the franchisor. (Also report the number of existing company-owned outlets that are sold to a franchisee in Column 7 of Table 4).

(E) In column 5, state the total number of franchised outlets that were terminated in each state during each fiscal year. For purposes of this section, "termination" means the franchisor's termination of a franchise agreement prior to the end of its term and without providing any consideration to the franchisee (whether by payment or forgiveness or assumption of debt).

(F) In column 6, state the total number of non-renewals in each state during each fiscal year. For purposes of this section, "non-renewal" occurs when the franchise agreement for a franchised outlet is not renewed at the end of its term.

(G) In column 7, state the total number of franchised outlets reacquired by the franchisor in each state during each fiscal year. For purposes of this section, a "reacquisition" means the franchisor's acquisition for consideration (whether by payment or forgiveness or assumption of debt) of a franchised outlet during its term. (Also report franchised outlets reacquired by the franchisor in column 5 of Table 4).

(H) In column 8, state the total number of outlets in each state not operating as one of the franchisor's outlets at the end of each fiscal year for reasons other than termination, non-renewal, or reacquisition by the franchisor.

(I) In column 9, state the total number of franchised outlets in each state at the end of the fiscal year.

(iii) Disclose, in the following tabular form, the status of company-owned outlets located in each state for each of the franchisor's last three fiscal years. A sample Item 20(4) Table is attached as appendix E to this part.

ITEM 20 TABLE NO. 4

Status of Company-Owned Outlets

For years [   ] to [   ]

Column 1 State	Column 2 Year	Column 3 Outlets at Start of Year	Column 4 Outlets Opened	Column 5 Outlets Reac- quired From Franchisee	Column 6 Outlets Closed	Column 7 Outlets Sold to Franchisee	Column 8 Outlets at End of the Year
	2004						
	2005						
	2006						
	2004						
	2005						
	2006						
Totals	2004						
	2005						
	2006						

(A) In column 1, list each state with one or more company-owned outlets.

(B) In column 2, state the last three fiscal years.

(C) In column 3, state the total number of company-owned outlets in each state at the start of the fiscal year.

(D) In column 4, state the total number of company-owned outlets opened in each state during each fiscal year.

(E) In column 5, state the total number of franchised outlets reacquired from franchisees in each state during each fiscal year.

(F) In column 6, state the total number of company-owned outlets closed in each state during each fiscal year. Include both actual closures and instances when an outlet ceases to operate under the franchisor's trademark.

(G) In column 7, state the total number of company-owned outlets sold to franchisees in each state during each fiscal year.

(H) In column 8, state the total number of company-owned outlets operating in each state at the end of each fiscal year.

(3) Disclose, in the following tabular form, projected new franchised and company-owned outlets. A sample Item 20(5) Table is attached as appendix F to this part.

ITEM 20 TABLE NO. 5

Projected Openings As Of [Last Day of Last Fiscal Year]

Column 1 State	Column 2 Franchise Agreements Signed But Outlet Not Opened	Column 3 Projected New Franchised Outlet In The Next Fiscal Year	Column 4 Projected New Company-Owned Outlet In the Next Fiscal Year
Total			

(i) In column 1, list each state where one or more franchised or company-owned outlets are located or are projected to be located.

(ii) In column 2, state the total number of franchise agreements that had been signed for new outlets to be located in each state as of the end of the previous fiscal year where the outlet had not yet opened.

(iii) In column 3, state the total number of new franchised outlets in each state projected to be opened during the next fiscal year.

(iv) In column 4, state the total number of new company-owned outlets in each state that are projected to be opened during the next fiscal year.

(4) Disclose the names of all current franchisees and the address and telephone number of each of their outlets. Alternatively, disclose this information for all franchised outlets in the state, but if these franchised outlets total fewer than 100, disclose this information for franchised outlets from contiguous states and then the next closest states until at least 100 franchised outlets are listed.

(5) Disclose the name, city and state, and current business telephone number, or if unknown, the last known home telephone number of every franchisee who had an outlet terminated, canceled, not renewed, or otherwise voluntarily or involuntarily ceased to do business under the franchise agreement during the most recently completed fiscal year or who has not communicated with the franchisor within 10 weeks of the disclosure document issuance date.[10] State in immediate conjunction with this information: "If you buy this franchise, your contact information may be disclosed to other buyers when you leave the franchise system."

(6) If a franchisor is selling a previously-owned franchised outlet now under its control, disclose the following additional information for that outlet for the last five fiscal years. This information may be attached as an addendum to a disclosure document, or, if disclosure has already been made, then in a supplement to the previously furnished disclosure document.

(i) The name, city and state, current business telephone number, or if unknown, last known home telephone number of each previous owner of the outlet;

____

[10] Franchisors may substitute alternative contact information at the request of the former franchisee, such as a home address, post office address, or a personal or business email address.

(ii) The time period when each previous owner controlled the outlet;

(iii) The reason for each previous change in ownership (for example, termination, non-renewal, voluntary transfer, ceased operations); and

(iv) The time period(s) when the franchisor retained control of the outlet (for example, after termination, non-renewal, or reacquisition).

(7) Disclose whether franchisees signed confidentiality clauses during the last three fiscal years. If so, state the following: "In some instances, current and former franchisees sign provisions restricting their ability to speak openly about their experience with [name of franchise system]. You may wish to speak with current and former franchisees, but be aware that not all such franchisees will be able to communicate with you." Franchisors may also disclose the number and percentage of current and former franchisees who during each of the last three fiscal years signed agreements that include confidentiality clauses and may disclose the circumstances under which such clauses were signed.

(8) Disclose, to the extent known, the name, address, telephone number, email address, and Web address (to the extent known) of each trademark-specific franchisee organization associated with the franchise system being offered, if such organization:

(i) Has been created, sponsored, or endorsed by the franchisor. If so, state the relationship between the organization and the franchisor (for example, the organization was created by the franchisor, sponsored by the franchisor, or endorsed by the franchisor).

(ii) Is incorporated or otherwise organized under state law and asks the franchisor to be included in the franchisor's disclosure document during the next fiscal year. Such organizations must renew their request on an annual basis by submitting a request no later than 60 days after the close of the franchisor's fiscal year. The franchisor has no obligation to verify the organization's continued existence at the end of each fiscal year. Franchisors may also include the following statement: "The following independent franchisee organizations have asked to be included in this disclosure document."

(u) *Item 21: Financial Statements.* (1) Include the following financial statements prepared according to United States generally accepted accounting principles, as revised by any future United States government mandated accounting principles, or as permitted by the Securities and Exchange Commission. Except as provided in paragraph (u)(2) of this section, these financial statements must be audited by an independent certified public accountant using generally accepted United States auditing standards. Present the required financial statements in a tabular form that compares at least two fiscal years.

(i) The franchisor's balance sheet for the previous two fiscal year-ends before the disclosure document issuance date.

(ii) Statements of operations, stockholders equity, and cash flows for each of the franchisor's previous three fiscal years.

(iii) Instead of the financial disclosures required by paragraphs (u)(1)(i) and (ii) of this section, the franchisor may include financial statements of any of its affiliates if the affiliate's financial statements satisfy paragraphs (u)(1)(i) and (ii) of this section and the affiliate absolutely and unconditionally guarantees to assume the duties and obligations of the franchisor under the franchise agreement. The affiliate's guarantee must cover all of the franchisor's obligations to the franchisee, but need not extend to third parties. If this alternative is used, attach a copy of the guarantee to the disclosure document.

(iv) When a franchisor owns a direct or beneficial controlling financial interest in a subsidiary, its financial statements should reflect the financial condition of the franchisor and its subsidiary.

(v) Include separate financial statements for the franchisor and any subfranchisor, as well as for any parent that commits to perform post-sale obligations for the franchisor or guarantees the franchisor's obligations. Attach a copy of any guarantee to the disclosure document.

(2) A start-up franchise system that does not yet have audited financial

statements may phase-in the use of audited financial statements by providing, at a minimum, the following statements at the indicated times:

(i) The franchisor' first partial or full fiscal year selling franchises.	An unaudited opening balance sheet.
(ii) The franchisor' second fiscal year selling franchises.	Audited balance sheet opinion as of the end of the first partial or full fiscal year selling franchises.
(iii) The franchisor' third and subsequent fiscal years selling franchises.	All required financial statements for the previous fiscal year, plus any previously disclosed audited statements that still must be disclosed according to paragraphs (u)(1)(i) and (ii) of this section.

(iv) Start-up franchisors may phase-in the disclosure of audited financial statements, provided the franchisor:

(A) Prepares audited financial statements as soon as practicable.

(B) Prepares unaudited statements in a format that conforms as closely as possible to audited statements.

(C) Includes one or more years of unaudited financial statements or clearly and conspicuously discloses in this section that the franchisor has not been in business for three years or more, and cannot include all financial statements required in paragraphs (u)(1)(i) and (ii) of this section.

(v) *Item 22*: *Contracts*. Attach a copy of all proposed agreements regarding the franchise offering, including the franchise agreement and any lease, options, and purchase agreements.

(w) *Item 23*: *Receipts*. Include two copies of the following detachable acknowledgment of receipt in the following form as the last pages of the disclosure document:

(1) State the following:

RECEIPT

This disclosure document summarizes certain provisions of the franchise agreement and other information in plain language. Read this disclosure document and all agreements carefully.

If [name of franchisor] offers you a franchise, it must provide this disclosure document to you 14 calendar-days before you sign a binding agreement with, or make a payment to, the franchisor or an affiliate in connection with the proposed franchise sale.

If [name of franchisor] does not deliver this disclosure document on time or if it contains a false or misleading statement, or a material omission, a violation of federal law and state law may have occurred and should be reported to the Federal Trade Commission, Washington, D.C. 20580 and [state agency].

(2) Disclose the name, principal business address, and telephone number of each franchise seller offering the franchise.

(3) State the issuance date.

(4) If not disclosed in paragraph (a) of this section, state the name and address of the franchisor's registered agent authorized to receive service of process.

(5) State the following:

I received a disclosure document dated __________ that included the following Exhibits:

(6) List the title(s) of all attached Exhibits.

(7) Provide space for the prospective franchisee's signature and date.

(8) Franchisors may include any specific instructions for returning the receipt (for example, street address, email address, facsimile telephone number).

Subpart D—Instructions

§ 436.6 Instructions for preparing disclosure documents.

(a) It is an unfair or deceptive act or practice in violation of Section 5 of the FTC Act for any franchisor to fail to include the information and follow the instructions for preparing disclosure documents set forth in subpart C (basic disclosure requirements) and subpart D (updating requirements) of part 436. The Commission will enforce this provision according to the standards of liability under Sections 5, 13(b), and 19 of the FTC Act.

(b) Disclose all required information clearly, legibly, and concisely in a single document using plain English. The disclosures must be in a form that permits each prospective franchisee to store, download, print, or otherwise maintain the document for future reference.

(c) Respond fully to each disclosure Item. If a disclosure Item is not applicable, respond negatively, including a reference to the type of information required to be disclosed by the Item. Precede each disclosure Item with the appropriate heading.

(d) Do not include any materials or information other than those required or permitted by part 436 or by state law not preempted by part 436. For the sole purpose of enhancing the prospective franchisee's ability to maneuver through an electronic version of a disclosure document, the franchisor may include scroll bars, internal links, and search features. All other features (e.g., multimedia tools such as audio, video, animation, pop-up screens, or links to external information) are prohibited.

(e) Franchisors may prepare multistate disclosure documents by including non-preempted, state-specific information in the text of the disclosure document or in Exhibits attached to the disclosure document.

(f) Subfranchisors shall disclose the required information about the franchisor, and, to the extent applicable, the same information concerning the subfranchisor.

(g) Before furnishing a disclosure document, the franchisor shall advise the prospective franchisee of the formats in which the disclosure document is made available, any prerequisites for obtaining the disclosure document in a particular format, and any conditions necessary for reviewing the disclosure document in a particular format.

(h) Franchisors shall retain, and make available to the Commission upon request, a sample copy of each materially different version of their disclosure documents for three years after the close of the fiscal year when it was last used.

(i) For each completed franchise sale, franchisors shall retain a copy of the signed receipt for at least three years.

§ 436.7 Instructions for updating disclosures.

(a) All information in the disclosure document shall be current as of the close of the franchisor's most recent fiscal year. After the close of the fiscal year, the franchisor shall, within 120 days, prepare a revised disclosure document, after which a franchise seller may distribute only the revised document and no other disclosure document.

(b) The franchisor shall, within a reasonable time after the close of each quarter of the fiscal year, prepare revisions to be attached to the disclosure document to reflect any material change to the disclosures included, or required to be included, in the disclosure document. Each prospective franchisee shall receive the disclosure document and the quarterly revisions for the most recent period available at the time of disclosure.

(c) If applicable, the annual update shall include the franchisor's first quarterly update, either by incorporating the quarterly update information into the disclosure document itself, or through an addendum.

(d) When furnishing a disclosure document, the franchise seller shall notify the prospective franchisee of any material changes that the seller knows or should have known occurred in the information contained in any financial performance representation made in Item 19 (section 436.5(s)).

(e) Information that must be audited pursuant to § 436.5(u) of this part need not be audited for quarterly revisions; provided, however, that the franchisor states in immediate conjunction with the information that such information was not audited.

Subpart E—Exemptions

§ 436.8 Exemptions.

(a) The provisions of part 436 shall not apply if the franchisor can establish any of the following:

(1) The total of the required payments, or commitments to make a required payment, to the franchisor or an affiliate that are made any time from before to within six months after commencing operation of the franchisee's business is less than $615.

(2) The franchise relationship is a fractional franchise.

(3) The franchise relationship is a leased department.

(4) The franchise relationship is covered by the Petroleum Marketing Practices Act, 15 U.S.C. 2801.

(5)(i) The franchisee's initial investment, excluding any financing received from the franchisor or an affiliate and excluding the cost of unimproved land, totals at least $1,233,000 and the prospective franchisee signs an acknowledgment verifying the grounds for the exemption. The acknowledgment shall state: "The franchise sale is for more than $1,233,000—excluding the cost of unimproved land and any financing received from the franchisor or an affiliate— and thus is exempted from the Federal Trade Commission's Franchise Rule disclosure requirements, pursuant to 16 CFR 436.8(a)(5)(i)"; [11] or

(ii) The franchisee (or its parent or any affiliates) is an entity that has been in business for at least five years and has a net worth of at least $6,165,000.

(6) One or more purchasers of at least a 50% ownership interest in the franchise: within 60 days of the sale, has been, for at least two years, an officer, director, general partner, individual with management responsibility for the offer and sale of the franchisor's franchises or the administrator of the franchised network; or within 60 days of the sale, has been, for at least two years, an owner of at least a 25% interest in the franchisor.

(7) There is no written document that describes any material term or aspect of the relationship or arrangement.

(b) For purposes of the exemptions set forth in this section, the Commission shall adjust the size of the monetary thresholds every fourth year based upon the Consumer Price Index. For purposes of this section, "Consumer Price Index" means the Consumer Price Index for all urban consumers published by the Department of Labor.

[72 FR 15544, Mar. 30, 2007, as amended at 77 FR 36150, June 18, 2012; 81 FR 31501, May 19, 2016; 85 FR 38791, June 29, 2020]

Subpart F—Prohibitions

§436.9 Additional prohibitions.

It is an unfair or deceptive act or practice in violation of Section 5 of the Federal Trade Commission Act for any franchise seller covered by part 436 to:

(a) Make any claim or representation, orally, visually, or in writing, that contradicts the information required to be disclosed by this part.

(b) Misrepresent that any person:

(1) Purchased a franchise from the franchisor or operated a franchise of the type offered by the franchisor.

(2) Can provide an independent and reliable report about the franchise or the experiences of any current or former franchisees.

(c) Disseminate any financial performance representations to prospective franchisees unless the franchisor has a reasonable basis and written substantiation for the representation at the time the representation is made, and the representation is included in Item 19 (§436.5(s)) of the franchisor's disclosure document. In conjunction with any such financial performance representation, the franchise seller shall also:

(1) Disclose the information required by §§436.5(s)(3)(ii)(B) and (E) of this part if the representation relates to the past performance of the franchisor's outlets.

(2) Include a clear and conspicuous admonition that a new franchisee's individual financial results may differ from the result stated in the financial performance representation.

(d) Fail to make available to prospective franchisees, and to the Commission upon reasonable request, written substantiation for any financial performance representations made in Item 19 (§436.5(s)).

(e) Fail to furnish a copy of the franchisor's disclosure document to a prospective franchisee earlier in the sales process than required under §436.2 of this part, upon reasonable request.

---

[11] The large franchise exemption applies only if at least one individual prospective franchisee in an investor-group qualifies for the exemption by investing at the threshold level stated in this section.

(f) Fail to furnish a copy of the franchisor's most recent disclosure document and any quarterly updates to a prospective franchisee, upon reasonable request, before the prospective franchisee signs a franchise agreement.

(g) Present for signing a franchise agreement in which the terms and conditions differ materially from those presented as an attachment to the disclosure document, unless the franchise seller informed the prospective franchisee of the differences at least seven days before execution of the franchise agreement.

(h) Disclaim or require a prospective franchisee to waive reliance on any representation made in the disclosure document or in its exhibits or amendments. Provided, however, that this provision is not intended to prevent a prospective franchisee from voluntarily waiving specific contract terms and conditions set forth in his or her disclosure document during the course of franchise sale negotiations.

(i) Fail to return any funds or deposits in accordance with any conditions disclosed in the franchisor's disclosure document, franchise agreement, or any related document.

Subpart G—Other Provisions

§ 436.10 Other laws and rules.

(a) The Commission does not approve or express any opinion on the legality of any matter a franchisor may be required to disclose by part 436. Further, franchisors may have additional obligations to impart material information to prospective franchisees outside of the disclosure document under Section 5 of the Federal Trade Commission Act. The Commission intends to enforce all applicable statutes and rules.

(b) The FTC does not intend to preempt the franchise practices laws of any state or local government, except to the extent of any inconsistency with part 436. A law is not inconsistent with part 436 if it affords prospective franchisees equal or greater protection, such as registration of disclosure documents or more extensive disclosures.

§ 436.11 Severability.

If any provision of this part is stayed or held invalid, the remainder will stay in force.

APPENDIX A TO PART 436—SAMPLE ITEM 10 TABLE—SUMMARY OF FINANCING OFFERED

SUMMARY OF FINANCING OFFERED

Item Financed	Source of Financing	Down Payment	Amount Financed	Term (Yrs)	Interest Rate	Monthly Payment	Prepay Penalty	Security Required	Liability Upon Default	Loss of Legal Right on Default
Initial Fee										
Land/Constr										
Leased Space										
Equip. Lease										
Equip. Purchase										
Opening Inventory										
Other Financing										

APPENDIX B TO PART 436—SAMPLE ITEM 20(1) TABLE—SYSTEMWIDE OUTLET
SUMMARY

Systemwide Outlet Summary
For years 2004 to 2006

Column 1 Outlet Type	Column 2 Year	Column 3 Outlets at the Start of the Year	Column 4 Outlets at the End of the Year	Column 5 Net Change
Franchised	2004	859	1,062	+ 203
	2005	1,062	1,296	+ 234
	2006	1,296	2,720	+ 1,424
Company Owned	2004	125	145	+ 20
	2005	145	76	-69
	2006	76	141	+ 65
Total Outlets	2004	984	1,207	+ 223
	2005	1,207	1,372	+ 165
	2006	1,372	2,861	+ 1,489

APPENDIX C TO PART 436—SAMPLE ITEM 20(2) TABLE—TRANSFERS OF FRANCHISED
OUTLETS

Transfers of Franchised Outlets from Franchisees to New
Owners (other than the Franchisor)
For years 2004 to 2006

Column 1 State	Column 2 Year	Column 3 Number of Trans- fers
NC	2004	1
	2005	0
	2006	2
SC	2004	0

Transfers of Franchised Outlets from Franchisees to New
Owners (other than the Franchisor)
For years 2004 to 2006

Column 1 State	Column 2 Year	Column 3 Number of Trans- fers
	2005	0
	2006	2
Total	2004	1
	2005	0
	2006	4

APPENDIX D TO PART 436—SAMPLE ITEM 20(3) TABLE—STATUS OF FRANCHISE
OUTLETS

Status of Franchise Outlets
For years 2004 to 2006

Column 1 State	Column 2 Year	Column 3 Outlets at Start of Year	Column 4 Outlets Opened	Column 5 Termi- nations	Column 6 Non-Re- newals	Column 7 Reacquired by Franchisor	Column 8 Ceased Op- erations- Other Rea- sons	Column 9 Outlets at End of the Year
AL	2004	10	2	1	0	0	1	10
	2005	11	5	0	1	0	0	15
	2006	15	4	1	0	1	2	15
AZ	2004	20	5	0	0	0	0	25
	2005	25	4	1	0	0	2	26
	2006	26	4	0	0	0	0	30
Totals	2004	30	7	1	0	0	1	35

ABOUT THE AUTHOR
FRANCHISE ATTORNEY HOUSTON BARNES

Houston Barnes, Founder of BarnesLaw, is a distinguished expert in the franchise industry, celebrated for his strategic insights. His career began as Vice President of a startup medical device company, which expanded globally under his leadership. After exiting the company, Houston transitioned into the dynamic world of franchising, where he quickly made his mark by collaborating closely with franchisors to master the intricacies of the industry.

Over time, Houston shifted his focus to exclusively representing franchisees, becoming a trusted advisor in reviewing and negotiating thousands of franchise agreements. His dedication to franchisees has earned him widespread recognition, with his work benefiting clients across a variety of sectors.

Houston's influence extends beyond the legal field. From being an invited guest at the White House and dining with sitting presidents and dignitaries, to international travel, Houston has a diverse and worldly view of entrepreneurship. Houston is frequent guest on leading industry podcasts and a sought-after speaker, and he is widely regarded as an authoritative voice in franchise law.

Known for his hands-on approach, Houston provides his clients with tailored, strategic advice, whether navigating the complexities of franchise disclosure documents or negotiating high-stakes agreements. His clients benefit from his comprehensive understanding of the franchise landscape and his commitment to personalized representation.

Houston earned degrees in both Business and Law from Southern Methodist University and the University of North Carolina, graduating with honors and cum laude distinctions. Outside of his professional achievements, Houston is a proud father of two sons and a daughter, who are the center of his world.